D0586011

Only Birds and Fools

Only Birds and Fools

Flight Engineer, Avro Lancaster, World War II

J. Norman Ashton, DFC

Airlife
England

Copyright © 2000 J. Norman Ashton

First Published in the UK in 2000
by Airlife Publishing Ltd

British Library Cataloguing in Publication Data
A catalogue record for this book
is available from the British Library

ISBN 1 84037 123 4

The information in this book is true and complete to the best
of our knowledge. All recommendations are made without any
guarantee on the part of the Publisher, who also disclaims any
liability incurred in connection with the use of this data or specific details.

All rights reserved. No part of this book may be reproduced or
transmitted in any form or by any means, electronic or
mechanical including photocopying, recording or by any
information storage and retrieval system, without permission
from the Publisher in writing.

Typeset by Phoenix Typesetting, Ilkley, West Yorkshire
Printed in England by St Edmundsbury Press Ltd., Bury St Edmunds, Suffolk.

Airlife Publishing Ltd

101 Longden Road, Shrewsbury, SY3 9EB England.
E-mail: airlife@airlifebooks.com
Web site: www.airlifebooks.com

PREFACE

I first heard the stories described in this book when I was a boy. Having tired of Goldilocks, I would listen spellbound to my father's tales of adventures with Reg Bunten, Bill Bailey and Corky Corcoran as they rode through the night sky inside a black charger called W-William to wreak vengeance on Nazi Germany. Theirs was a world lit only by searchlights, tracer bullets and the green and red fairy lights of target indicators. A world shared with mischievous gremlins and goblinesque night-fighters. I was enthralled.

But I was also horrified. I knew the casualty figures. I could do the sums. I knew my father was lucky to have survived the 54 sorties he flew as a Flight Engineer in Lancaster bombers between 1943 and 1945. I knew it and he knew it, and it made us close.

Despite the loss of friends, the war years were the best of my father's life; as if through witnessing death and oppression, he came to doubly value life and freedom. He earned the peace he fought for and did not squander its rewards. After the war he returned to his home town and became a devoted father of five children. We have our own private memories of him during those years. Now, with the publication of this book, we also have a permanent record of a crucial earlier chapter in his life.

This book was first drafted in 1945, at a time when understatement was fashionable. But I have resisted the temptation to make stylistic changes to bring the text into line with current trends. I felt it more important to preserve my father's manner of expression, which itself contributes to the historical record.

My father typed the original manuscript on a clunky Yost. He then used his skills as a Master Printer to bind the sheets and original photographs into two hardback volumes, their titles inlaid in gold. The books then passed from hand to hand among his old RAF colleagues. He took great delight in re-igniting memories – both joyful and sad – of those important years, and would have been thrilled to witness this wider publication of his work. I am so very proud of him. In every sense.

STEVE ASHTON
September 1999

The author, J. Norman Ashton, DFC

FOREWORD

In this book of wartime recollections, I have tried to give a faithful account of my experiences as a flight engineer on Lancaster aircraft of Bomber Command. The primary purpose of the book was to form a personal record of those stirring times – a safeguard against the inevitable day when I would no longer be able to recall events or identify, with certainty, once-familiar faces on squadron photographs. There was then, neither the necessity nor the wish to garnish the stories and it is in that original form that I now present them, except that to avoid repetition, I have on occasion blended certain separate incidents into a continuous story.

The task of compiling the material was not an easy one, for I had to rely to a great extent on my memory – with promptings from brief and infrequent diary entries, my flying log book, and a collection of photographs and souvenirs. Memories, I know, can sometimes play strange tricks and I realise that the book may contain occasional errors in references to incidents, persons or dates. If that is the case, I apologise in advance and assure the offended that every story has been written with the best of intentions.

J. NORMAN ASHTON
20 March 1961

CONTENTS

CHAPTER ONE
SITUATION VACANT

The boys were obviously not impressed and they drifted slowly back to the Hudsons which stood jacked and trestled in the far corner of the hangar. I turned again to read the notice on the Met. Flight gen board: it was the usual Air Ministry effort, recently adorned with oily smudges from inquisitive fingers.

Shorn of Service jargon, the notice intimated that the Royal Air Force required flight engineers for the new four-engined bombers which were rolling off the production lines, and applications were invited from airmen already trained as engine fitters. Briefly, the scheme was to subject volunteers to high-pressure instruction on a particular type of aircraft; teach them how to operate a gun-turret in the event of an emergency; issue brevet, sergeant's stripes and flying kit to successful candidates and give them a certain amount of flying experience before being projected at high velocity into the night skies over the Third Reich. There seemed every promise of an exciting career but no guarantee as to how long it would last.

The engine fitters of 1405 Met. Flight had cushy jobs at Aldergrove, Northern Ireland, and could rightly claim to be doing invaluable work by keeping the Hudsons and Spitfires flying. But suppose all the engine fitters in the RAF adopted the same attitude? I just couldn't turn away and laugh the whole thing off. A few weeks before, on the night of 30 May 1942, I had been thrilled by the news of the raid on Cologne by 1000 bombers. That, thought I, was the life for a man: no phoney war, but just taking the Hun by the throat and shaking him. The question resolved itself; was I content to let others fight the battles or was I man enough to do my own fighting? To any Briton with technical knowledge, a good medical category, and a conscience, there could be only one answer.

Volunteering for aircrew duties, meant just that. There was not the slightest degree of compulsion or intimidation. Indeed, the keen types often felt that the 'Airworks' was doing everything it possibly

1

could to stop them getting into aircrew. Even at St Athan, the new trainees – distinguished by the white flash on the front of their service caps – were assured, time after time, that any airman who wished to change his mind could leave the course at once and return to his unit. As I listened to these appeals to the half-hearted, I thought how neatly the words of Shakespeare's *Henry V* fitted the situation:

> 'That he which hath no stomach to this fight,
> Let him depart; his passport shall be made,
> And crowns for convoy put into his purse:'

The 16th of November 1942 was my thirtieth birthday and the RAF generously recognised the occasion by advising me that I was to proceed to No. 4 School of Technical Training, St Athan, South Wales, at my earliest convenience. Coincidences had always interested me and none more than when I learned that a home-town friend of pre-war days was also en route for German skies. Jack Osborne had also volunteered for flight engineer and we travelled down to St Athan together; although I was ten years older than Jack, we had a great deal in common and decided to stick together as far as the RAF, the enemy and fate would allow. We made great plans for the future and were confident that honour and distinction would be ours in the fullness of time.

The training hangar at St Athan – known as the 'Flannel Factory' – was a huge place, elaborately equipped and efficiently organised. There were courses for flight engineers on Halifax, Lancaster, Stirling, Sunderland and Catalina aircraft, and the component parts of these kites lay thick on the floor and walls of the hangar. The training staff was a team of enthusiasts and every effort was made to ensure that the courses were interesting and enjoyable, as well as instructive. I had set my heart on flying in Lancasters; perhaps influenced in my preference by the horrible rumours circulating that the casualty rate on 'Halibags' was frightful, and that the 'Flying Solenoid' (as the Stirling was known, because of its numerous electrical gadgets) was a sitting target for enemy night fighters. As for the flying boats, I just wasn't interested, I wanted action and excitement, not dreary sea-stooges; so I was quite relieved when I was chosen for the Lanc. course.

The study of aircraft had long been a favourite hobby of mine and at St Athan I was able to exploit my enthusiasm to the full. We ran the whole gamut: engine and airframe construction; hydraulic, electrical, fuel and compressed-air systems; engine handling; propellers; flight drills; oxygen system; repairs in flight; and dozens of other interesting subjects. For nine weeks – including a memorable week at the Avro works – I thought, talked and dreamed of Lancasters. My love for them became fanatical. They began to live.

I felt confident that I would do well in the final examination, everything was going fine and then towards the end of the course I had severe blood-poisoning in my arm and suffered considerable pain and inconvenience. I was in bad shape when I took the exams and feared that I would not make the grade. It was, I thought, the end of all my dreams.

Later, the results were announced and I was overjoyed to learn that I had obtained second highest marks. I was through!

Life at St Athan had been good. New friends had been made and a long-standing friendship sealed. Furthermore, for what it was worth, an Indian friend on the course had 'read my palm' and solemnly assured me that I had nothing to fear for the future. I would still be alive and well when the war ended.

The only dark spot had been that Jimmy ('Grindlestone') Green, my bosom pal in the piping days of peace, had fractured his spine when making a parachute drop at night. He was still alive, but his paratroop days were over and I knew that he would be bitterly disappointed. There had been a third pal to make up the 'Three Musketeers' in the old days, but Bill ('Believe-you-me') Smith had been killed early in 1942, when the engines of his aircraft failed on take off.

Feeling proud of my new Flight Engineer's brevet, I started the Air Gunnery Course at Stormydown in high spirits. The superior, 'lords-of-the-air' attitude of the Bomber Boys was already beginning to seep into my system. I felt good. The course could be as tough as the instructors cared to make it. I would pass.

They gave us Browning guns, fighter tactics, aircraft recognition, sighting, pyrotechnics, gun-turret systems, gun theory, gun harmonising, gun stoppages, gun everything! I revelled in it. I expected top marks in the examinations, and got them.

Whilst sewing on my sergeant's stripes, I pondered on the change of outlook. Whence came the confidence and self-pride? The more I thought about it, the more I became convinced that the RAF purposely instilled into aircrew trainees the knowledge that they would be the finest men, flying the finest aircraft, in the finest service

3

in the world. And surely, that was the spirit which won battles and wars.

'Aircrew Fitness Course' – I didn't really like the sound of that. It smacked of solid work in the gymnasium, barbarous assault-courses, and aching limbs. Besides, I was now a flight engineer and wanted to get airborne as soon as possible. On arrival at Binbrook, however, I realised that this was another of the RAF's little schemes for the welfare of aircrew types. The fitness, I found, was mental rather than physical. As a preliminary, we were given seven day's leave and I appreciated the chance to see my people before I started flying.

Our short stay at Binbrook was spent in making the acquaintance of the other categories of aircrew. These were real flying personnel, with kit-bags full of flying-clothing, and log-books containing flying times. We engineers were very subdued as we listened to the general conversation. The other fellows were already in crews, having completed their training at Operational Training Units on Wellington or Whitley aircraft, whilst we had flown only on occasional air tests; several of the engineers had never been airborne. However, we were all crewed-up a few days later and there was a big improvement in the general atmosphere. I joined a crew skippered by the Australian, F/O Jackie Burkhart, which included Terry Hoy, navigator, Alan Washbrook, bomb aimer, and 'Jacko' Jackson, the Canadian rear gunner. I was interested to learn that 'Washy' was a relative of the famous Lancashire batsman, Cyril Washbrook.

Binbrook also gave us the opportunity of learning the customs and routine of life in a Sergeants' Mess. We found this very different from the Airmen's Mess and NAAFI days of the past, and soon noticed that bomber aircrew were intended to be the best-fed personnel in the British Forces.

On the last day of the 'Fitness Course', we, the crew, slowly made our way from the Mess to our sleeping quarters. It was a glorious spring evening. A cloudless sky, coppered by the setting sun, a gentle breeze lending freshness to the air, and over all a sense of peace and tranquility. We stopped for a while, in silence. The war seemed far away.

Then, as we gazed skywards, a few black specks appeared on the horizon and we heard the faint drone which heralds the approach of aircraft. As we watched, the specks grew bigger, their number increased and the faint drone became the dull roar of heavy bombers. They were heading in a south-easterly direction, flying very high and still climbing. The sky now seemed full of the grim, black shapes and the throbbing beat of their powerful engines went straight to the pit of my stomach. This was the first time I had seen the 'heavies' going to war and I was strangely impressed. I had wanted excitement and action, aggressive action. Well, there it was.

We looked at each other. We had the same thoughts: hundreds of aircraft, each with a crew of seven men on board, carrying a load of death and destruction to the heart of Germany. Hundreds going out, how many would return? In a few weeks' time the scene would be the same – with the exception that we seven would be flying in our own bomber, heading in a south-easterly direction, flying very high and still climbing. Would *we* return?

CHAPTER TWO
DRESS REHEARSAL

There was a great shaking of hands and slapping of backs when I saw Jack and the rest of the St Athan boys at Lindholme; they had gone ahead when I was delayed by my poisoned arm and it seemed years since we last met – it was, in fact, six weeks. The boys had already been at Heavy Conversion Unit a fortnight and were hoping to be posted to their squadrons, for operational flying, in about ten days' time. They had enjoyed their stay at Lindholme and were loud in their praises of Doncaster as a town which catered for the airman on his off-duty wanderings. The flying training itself was grand fun, though there had been incidents. Walker's aircraft had pranged on landing and was lying with a broken back on the far side of the aerodrome; another chap had to 'feather' an engine which caught fire on take off; someone else burst a tyre as they were touching down, the subsequent behaviour of the aircraft proving highly entertaining to the crew and a few lucky spectators. All very interesting but not exactly cheering to a newcomer.

As befitted veterans of fourteen days' flying, they were full of good advice and when I left them my head was buzzing with a welter of conflicting evidence. On one point only were they unanimous, the aircraft were 'killers' and ready for the scrap-heap.

One of the first tasks at Lindholme was to report to Stores to draw flying kit, plus a kit-bag to hold it. After carefully marking the new kit-bag with number, rank and name, I began to stow away my recently acquired flying clothing. With a thrill of pride, each article was examined: aircrew battledress; leather helmet, complete with microphone, headphones and oxygen mask; lambskin flying boots; woollen, silk, chamois and leather gloves; white sweater; wool and rayon underwear; corrected-lens goggles (a sop to my suspect night-vision); one-piece flying suit; long woollen stockings; floating torch; and a silver-plated whistle. The rest of the crew looked on in amuse-

6

The author in flying kit

ment. They had long since passed the stage when kitting-up was an exciting business, and warned me that I would soon be tired of carrying the extra weight around.

A card game was in progress and, after fastening the kit-bag, I sat on my bed and took stock of the men who were to be my companions. The crew arrangements made at Binbrook had been unscrambled on our arrival at Lindholme and I had thrown in my lot with an all-sergeant crew. We had been together for only a few days but already I seemed to know everything about them. Service life was a high-pressure existence and friendships were formed in a remarkably short time; the chance acquaintance of one day was quite often the bosom friend of the next.

The slim, good looking fellow with the lazy smile, was Reg Bunten,

R. J. 'Reg' Bunten
(pilot)

The crew of

W-William

J. Norman Ashton
(flight engineer)

R. T. Boys
(wireless operator)

D. 'Doug' Wilkinson
(rear gunner)

E. C. 'Bill' Bailey
(navigator)

K. B. 'Corky' Corcoran
(bomb aimer)

E. 'Eddie' Smith
(mid-upper gunner)

the pilot. He had been trained in Florida on single-engined Harvards and subsequently, in England, on twin-engined Oxford and Whitley aircraft. Reg, I thought, would be cool, confident and capable, and equal to any situation which might arise.

Seated next to Reg was the navigator, Bill Bailey. A typical Londoner, bright and breezy as a Cockney sparrow. Trained in Canada, recently married and very much in love, Bill would probably have a steadying influence on the rest of the crew.

A deep chortle drew my attention to Corky Corcoran, our Canada-trained bomb aimer. A Yorkshireman, and proud of it, Corky was an amazing person. He was deeply religious and I found it hard to reconcile the undoubted sincerity of his beliefs with his impending participation in the ugly business of mass slaughter. Corky was a gen-man on rail travel and should it be our unfortunate lot to be wandering around Germany, sans aircraft, he would probably be able to arrange a trouble-free journey back to the Motherland in a First Class compartment.

A haze of tobacco smoke hid the face of the wireless operator, Reg Boys, but I could easily picture his good-natured smile and merry eyes. Solid type. Dependable, methodical and had probably never heard of the word 'panic'. No worries about the capabilities of Reg Boys.

Our two gunners, Eddie Smith and Doug Wilkinson, sat with their backs towards me but there was no mistaking their identities. Eddie, the mid-upper gunner, was tall and had the bearing of a typical Canadian. Hailing from Sioux Lookout, he had worked with an airline company, had been a gold miner, trapper, and a guide on hunting and fishing expeditions. Entirely fearless, was my guess, and a man to have around when things got dicey. Woe betide the night fighter pilot who was rash enough to get into Eddie's gunsight.

Doug was of smaller and sturdier build, and differed greatly in outlook. Yorkshire bred, he was often very quiet and busy with his own thoughts but, on occasion, would leap into the conversation and talk for hours. He would, I thought, sit behind those four Brownings in the rear turret without a qualm, and never would it occur to him that any Jerry could possibly catch him napping.

I could not have wished for better men. I liked them individually and collectively. There was youth and dash, tempered with responsibility and caution; a sense of skill and readiness to work for the well-being of all. A grand crew and I had not the slightest hesitation in facing the future in their company.

And what, I wondered, did they think of me? We had made friends readily enough but my capabilities in the air could only be assessed when we started flying. As a flight engineer, I was an unknown quantity but I was determined to make myself as efficient as possible.

My ruminations were cut short by the breaking up of the card game. The players finished their argument over the last hand, the lucky ones trousered their winnings, and all set course for bed. We were due to commence flying training on the morrow and an early night was indicated.

Strangely enough, my first trip in a heavy bomber was not in a Lancaster. For some reason, we were taught to fly Halifax aircraft before going on to Lancs. Rather disappointing but the fact remained that I was airborne. My log-book contained some flying hours at last, including some red-inked entries denoting night flying.

The crew was moulding itself into an efficient unit and we soon ironed out the inevitable snags and mistakes. Despite the grim warnings of the 'Athan' boys, we had very little trouble with the aircraft. The Lancasters, with their Merlin engines, exceeded even my expectations and I soon accustomed myself to moving the correct levers and pushing the correct buttons, at the correct time and in the correct manner. We did circuits-and-bumps, two- and three-engined flying, flapless landings, overshoots, stalls, practice bombing, Gee stooges, and night cross-country flights. The final exercise was a 'Bullseye' and this was carried out in true operational style. We had a pukka briefing and were instructed to treat the whole thing with the seriousness of an actual operational mission. We had a trouble-free trip and confirmed the confidence we felt in ourselves, in each other, and in the type of aircraft we were to fly.

The dress rehearsal was over and all was set for the opening night. The RAF had expended valuable time and money on giving us the finest training and equipment in the world – they now expected results. The door to glory was wide open, and we were on the threshold.

CHAPTER THREE

W-FOR-WILLIAM

As the crew-coach accelerated down the road, we gave the thumbs-up sign to the Lindholme boys who were waving from the open windows. They were going on to join their squadrons at Binbrook and Waltham. The leave-taking had been cheery enough but the firm handshakes betrayed unspoken thoughts. From that moment, life became a day-to-day existence and we knew that many of us would never meet again. I was particularly sorry to say *Au revoir* to Andy Kelly, who had been with me on the Flight Mechanics' Course at Kirkham in 1940.

Our destination was Elsham Wolds, a wartime station and likely to be comparatively rough-and-ready, as indeed it was. We stood by the untidy pile of kit-bags, eyeing with dismay the Nissen hut which was to be our home for the next few months. Rather a come-down, we felt, after the luxury of previous billets. Still, we had the hut to ourselves and would be able to make it cosy. The kit was carried inside and we started to sort ourselves out. Beds were moved around until everyone was satisfied and then each wall-space was decorated according to individual taste. Pin-up girls and photographs of wives and sweethearts were in great favour, whilst I – the dedicated engineer – settled for a wizard cut-away diagram of a Lancaster.

We had arrived at Elsham, fully prepared to be thrown straight into the maelstrom of operational flying. That, however, was not the case. Number 103 Squadron had been given a week's stand-down and this gave us the chance to settle in without undue haste. The squadron, we learned, had been very busy and was now licking its wounds and preparing men and machines for an all-out assault on the Ruhr. 'Happy Valley', as it it was known to the crews, had long been a popular spot with Bomber Command and the introduction of new radar aids now made possible the complete destruction of the main cities of the Ruhr, with all that that meant to the Nazi war effort.

There was an air of keenness and vitality about the whole place, an ops 'drome of which we had heard so much during our training days. The trappings of war were all around us: long, low bomb trolleys trundling round the perimeter track; flak-torn aircraft under repair in the hangars; belts of operational ammo in the armoury; a recent battle-order pinned to the notice-board in the crew room; aiming-point photos displayed in the Intelligence Section; a sprinkling of medal ribbons on battledress blouses; rows of miniature bombs (denoting raids) painted on the sides of the aircraft; and the partially erased, but still readable, names of missing crews on the squadron crew-state board.

On joining a new unit, it was customary for members of a crew to report to their respective leaders and to meet the other boys in the section. They were then given all the latest gen and acquainted with the equipment and methods adopted by the particular section. At that

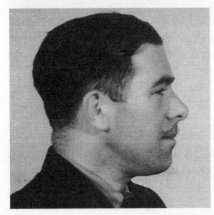

'Escape' photographs of the author. Airmen were issued with photographs in case they were forced to bale out over mainland Europe. These would then form the basis of false identification papers prepared by the Resistance.

time, however, this did not apply to flight engineers. They had neither leader nor section and the only person to take the slightest technical interest in them was the Squadron Engineering Officer. Usually, he was too busy with the maintenance of the aircraft to devote much time to flight engineers and they were left very much to their own devices. I soon realised that I would have to rely largely upon my own initiative and the advice of the more experienced fellows.

I drew a kit of tools and a torch from the squadron stores; parachute, harness and 'Mae West' from the parachute section; transferred my flying clothing to the locker room; and was all set for action.

Our early days with 103 Squadron were rather in the nature of an anti-climax. We were so eager to start operating and to make good as a crew, that it never occurred to us that things might not work out according to plan. Our first flight, a 'Bullseye' exercise, had to be abandoned when we were forced to 'feather' both starboard engines over the English Channel. True, we did return to base in good order and made a fine landing, but we were very disappointed.

The night of 23 May 1943 was the occasion of the heaviest raid of the war, up to that date, the target being the unfortunate town of Dortmund. It was also to have been our first sortie. To our dismay, we were not amongst those present. Complete failure of the flying instruments, whilst crossing the North Sea, resulted in a decision to jettison the bombs and abandon the mission.

How different from those wonderful dreams of ours! We felt thoroughly dejected. Compare our effort with that of another new crew with whom we were very friendly. Kenneth Breckon and his boys were attacked by fighters when approaching the target but managed to shoot their way out, with the loss of one engine – pressed-on and bombed – were again attacked by fighters, one of which was shot down in flames by the mid-upper gunner, the American George Ferrell, but only after the loss of another engine – reached the home coast, when a third engine caught fire – finally making a crash belly-landing, without a single casualty in the crew. Both Ken Breckon and George Ferrell were awarded the DFM. That, we thought, was something like a first mission.

After a good night's sleep, we reviewed the whole thing in the cold light of reason and felt that, after all, we had carefully weighed the circumstances and had made the right decision. We intended always to press home our attacks but, at the same time, realised that even in the heat of battle, valour must still be tempered with discretion.

Bomber Command – and the cause for which we were fighting – would be better served if we lived to complete a tour of operations, than if we threw away everything in a single night of glory. Provided, of course, that the choice was ours!

Two nights later, we regained our self-confidence. The target was Dusseldorf and we had a good trip. We flew with all fingers crossed for luck and heaved a sigh of relief when we sighted the hundreds of searchlight beams criss-crossing the target area – no abortive sortie this time! The effect of that first glimpse of a town undergoing the agony of a saturation raid was shattering. The fierce red glow of bursting bombs, the white shimmer of incendiaries, the brilliant glare of target indicators, the blinding flashes of the photo flares, the red-gold strings of 'flaming onions', and the whole witches' cauldron of fire and belching smoke, was like hell let loose. My mind was bludgeoned by the impact of it all.

It was all over in a few minutes: Reg made a good run-up; Corky picked out the target and pressed the bomb-tit; the aircraft shuddered as the bombs left the racks; Bill gave us a course and we turned for home. Our operational tour had started.

Our next trip was destined to become legendary. The target was Wuppertal (the name given to the twin-towns, Barmen and Elberfeld), famous for its suspended mono-railway system. The route took us through the gap between the defended areas of Cologne and Dusseldorf. At least, we were glibly assured by Intelligence of the existence of a gap. As all crews present on that memorable night agreed, the 'gap' proved to be the concentrated aiming-point of the combined defences of both cities. We ran the gauntlet with faint hopes of getting through in one piece, the flak was so thick that we could almost have put our wheels down and taxied across! The 'Reaper' was busy on all sides but we managed to evade his chopper. The raid was very successful but the comments of returned crews were unprintable. Everyone felt that the Intelligence bods had really let the side down. Chesterton's crew summed up the feelings of all engaged in the attack, when they introduced a little song with the apt title, 'Mythical Gap'. Sung to the tune of the Laurel-and-Hardy 'Cuckoo Song', it was soon adopted by the squadron. The following three verses, in particular, were sung with great gusto:

> 'Wuppertal. Wuppertal.
> Mythical gap. Mythical gap.
> 'Twixt Cologne and Dusseldorf
> There isn't a gap at all.

'We went there, one Friday night,
Oh, what a trip. Oh, what a sight.
Bags of flak and bags of light,
    But there wasn't a gap at all.

'We'll go back, we don't know when,
Now we've got all the pukka gen,
Intelligence have boobed again,
    There isn't a gap at all!'

We had done four trips when we got our first leave and I went home feeling quite a veteran. It was a common saying in Bomber Command that any crew completing four operations had an even chance of finishing their tour. Whatever the value of that statement, I did feel that we were showing progress and had got what it takes to make a good crew.

Whilst on leave, I met Jack's people and learned that he was still at Lindholme, having had a spell of illness which necessitated his removal to hospital. Our early decision to stick together was not working out as planned. Still, there was the chance that he might be posted to Elsham at a later date.

On our return from leave, Reg went on a week's course to the Rolls-Royce works and the rest of us expected a nice scrounge. This did not materialise. The engineer of one of the new crews was sick and I flew in his place on trips to Cologne and Gelsenkirchen. Bob Cant had a good crew and I enjoyed flying with them but their aircraft, 'U-Uncle', was a rather aged chariot which just managed to stagger up to 17,000 feet. Bob seemed quite satisfied with the altitude but I felt too near the deck for comfort – it seemed strange to be milling around in the company of Halifaxes, Wellingtons and Stirlings; usually, we Lancaster types were far above them.

Eddie and Bill also did a couple of spare trips. Bill had a hectic time with Chesterton and company on the Oberhausen raid. They were heavily engaged over the target and had the elevator controls damaged by flak. The aircraft practically stood on its tail, being un-decided whether to resume its normal attitude or turn over on to its back. 'Ches' eventually regained control and all was well but the incident shook the boys – especially as the bomb load was still on board. Eddie gave the rest of us a worrying time. We had been lying awake in bed waiting for him to return from a trip and it seemed hours before the genial Canadian swept into the billet with a cheery 'Hiyah, fellows!'. They had landed rather late and he had rounded off the

103 Squadron, Elsham Wolds

night with a game of snooker in the Mess. We, who had imagined the poor fellow in dire distress, were not amused and he was soundly reproved for his thoughtlessness.

When Reg returned from his course, we were given a brand-new aircraft which had just arrived on the squadron. At the same time there was an important addition to the crew. 'Joe' was a tiny fellow with a man-sized job, as fine a mascot as ever graced a Lancaster. Made of wool and looking every inch an airman, he was charged with the task of ensuring the safe return of crew and aircraft – no easy assignment, in view of the forces mustered to effect the early demise of both.

There it was – a brand-new Lancaster III, with the new Packard Merlin engines, and not a blemish from the clear-vision panel in the nose to the flash-eliminators on the rear turret Brownings. What a kite! And ours, for keeps! No more grumbles about sloppy controls, low oil-pressures, sluggish turrets or poor performance. No more flying old aircraft in which other crews had made reputations. We now had the finest bombing aircraft that the world could produce and had the opportunity of building up a reputation of our own. The riggers had just finished painting the squadron letters 'PM' and aircraft letter 'W' on the sides of the fuselage, and we surveyed their handiwork.

'W' – 'W-for-William' – Bunten and crew in 'W-for-William' – I liked the sound of the name, there was something whimsical about it. I wondered what sort of a future we would have together. Would he prove to be a 'jeep', giving trouble on every trip, or would he go from strength to strength, a delight to fly and a credit to his crew and squadron? Somehow, I felt that we would grow to love 'William' and that our chances of completing a tour had been doubled.

The ground staff boys walked towards us and there were introductions all round. Ernie, Bill, Taffy and Gar appeared to be capable and enthusiastic types, and I was confident we would have a good team – aircrew, aircraft, ground crew and mascot. The sergeant had already ground-tested the engines and was perfectly satisfied with them. In fact, everything was wizard. And, what is more, he informed us that he had never lost a 'W', they always came back – sometimes badly battered but, nevertheless, they came back. It was good to know.

We all hoped that 'William' would have something spectacular in the way of targets for his first trip. He had behaved magnificently on air-test and we were anxious to introduce him to the exciting busi-

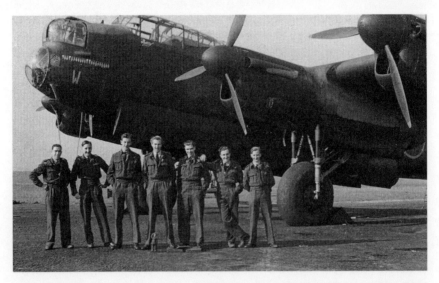

W-William and crew (from left to right): Norman Ashton, Corky Corcoran, Eddie Smith, Reg Bunten, Reg Boys, Doug Wilkinson and Bill Bailey. In front: Joe, the mascot.

ness of hammering the *Reich.* 'Joe' was also eager to be making a start.

One morning, Reg came out of 'C' Flight Office with a frown on his usually smiling face. He was obviously disappointed about something. We listened to his tale of woe and the disappointment became mutual. The squadron, with the exception of four crews, was on stand-down: the four crews were detailed for a mining trip; Bunten's crew was amongst those detailed.

We were furious. A mining trip? Bunten's crew on a mining trip? Surely, someone had blundered! Minelaying was a job for 'Wimpeys' or Hampdens, not Lancasters. In any case, why pick on a fully-fledged crew with seven ops to their credit? We couldn't have been more disgusted if we had been asked to take part in a 'Nickel' or a 'Bullseye'.

Still, the job had to be done, so we made our preparations for a nice, easy stooge – probably be nothing more than a glorified cross-country. Eddie and Doug threatened to sleep throughout the trip but I knew that, as ever, they would be right on their toes, taking nothing for granted. Reg and Corky went into a huddle with the Bombing Leader and got the gen on the technique of sea-mining and the precautions to be taken. The briefing was short and the instructions

19

straightforward. Our mining area was off the mouth of the Gironde, in the Bay of Biscay, and the object of the trip was to promote maximum interference with the U-boats raiding our Atlantic convoys. Defences were negligible, weather would be ideal. Emphasis was laid on the need for accuracy during the run over the dropping area; altitude, heading, airspeed and rate of dropping must be correct. In the event of unfavourable conditions or uncertainty of position, mines were to be retained and brought back to base.

The outward journey was uneventful. After take-off, we climbed leisurely until we were at 16,000 feet crossing the French coast. All very pleasant and 'William' behaving like a perfect gentleman. We began to lose height as we neared Bordeaux and immediately ran into ten/tenths cloud, which still persisted as we turned towards the coast. The cloud base was about 2,000 feet and, once below that height, Corky was able to pin-point the tiny island from which we were to commence the run across the mouth of the river. Feeling very vulnerable, we turned on to the correct heading and levelled out.

The local inhabitants had been very considerate, making neither objection nor inquiry as to the nature of our visit. At least, that was the state of affairs up to the moment when we committed ourselves to the run. Then, without further ado, the whole area blazed into a super edition of a Brock's Benefit Night. Scores of searchlights concentrated on poor 'William' and every gun on the Atlantic coast opened up. We felt extremely uncomfortable. Flak was never funny, but when conditions made it impossible to take evasive action, it became disconcerting, to say the least. Tracer streamed towards us from shore batteries, flak-ships, naval craft and machine-guns. At our altitude, they almost appeared to be firing down at us. The whole aircraft seemed to be wrapped in the flashes – like an ungainly Guy Fawkes perched awkwardly on a flickering bonfire. It was fantastic. We could hear, feel and smell the filthy stuff belting against the aircraft but nothing untoward happened. Doug complained that all the guns were pointing at his turret and he swore that he could see hand-grenades whizzing past!

We flew straight and level, dropping our mines at intervals, for what seemed hours rather than minutes. Then, with a sigh of relief, Corky gave the OK, I opened up the engines to climbing power, and Reg pulled 'William' into the clouds. As I turned to synchronise the engines by watching the 'sheen' on the prop blades, a sinister black shape whistled past the starboard wing-tip. A Junkers 88! I snapped a warning through to the gunners. Doug acknowledged and then the staccato bark of twin Brownings in action crackled over the intercom. Streaks of tracer from the mid-upper turret flashed away to port, like red-hot needles stabbing into a bale of cotton wool – Eddie was having a go. Apparently, he had just switched on his mike to reply to my warning, when he spotted another hostile aircraft within range and had given him a short burst. In a few minutes all was quiet again. The interfering '88s' had lost us in the cloud, the flak types had called it a day, and the searchlight beams had dropped back into their reflectors for the night. We climbed to a respectable height and set course for home. 'William' was in grand form and the 'glorified cross-country' had proved really interesting. We felt satisfied with the night's work.

Next morning, we pottered round to dispersal to see how 'William' had fared on his maiden trip. The riggers grinned as they pointed out the flak-holes in the tailplane and the engine-nacelles – 'William' was operational, with battle-scars to prove it. He seemed to blush with pride when I glanced up at the little white parachute and mine, newly painted on the port side of his nose. The team had scored its first victory.

I climbed inside and went up to the cockpit to have a word with

Avro Lancaster

21

'Joe'. He had enjoyed the trip and hoped that we fully appreciated his magic powers. His position behind Reg's seat, just below the Perspex canopy, was ideal – a mascot had to have a clear view in all directions and be able to keep a watchful eye on mischievous gremlins.

The boys made several suggestions for a crest or motto to be painted on the aircraft but it was decided that the simple 'W' was adornment enough. Later, we compromised by having our wives' or girl friends' names painted on the fuselage in the various crew positions.

Naturally, we were subjected to some leg-pulling because of our 'gift' trip but that didn't worry us. We had learned to respect the work of crews who regularly performed the rather dull but often dangerous task of laying mines in enemy waters.

I was chatting with the ground crew when the crew-coach rolled into dispersal. Reg and the boys had arrived, complete with flying kit – the squadron was operating that night and we were on the battle order. 'William' had not flown for a couple of days and we had to do an air-test – or NFT – before lunch. We had a busy day before us and I smiled as I thought of my early impressions of life on an operational squadron.

During my ground-training period, I had only a vague idea of the manner in which a bombing mission was carried out. There would be some sort of pre-arranged plan, of course, but the operation would probably begin by someone saying, 'OK, fellows, let's go and bomb Cologne!' The crews would pile out to the aircraft, nip smartly over to Cologne, bomb the first available factory, then stick the nose down and race home, pausing only to shoot down a few enemy fighters on the way. All over in four or five hours, followed by a long rest until some busybody thought up another target. Actually, nothing could have been further from the truth. A typical attack in strength by Bomber Command demanded the attention of aircrews for practically twenty-four hours, in addition to the time required by HQ staff to plan and co-ordinate the operation as a whole.

The ground crew had already finished their daily inspections, so we climbed into the aircraft and were off the deck by 1030 hours. We always put 'William' through his paces on air-test. Each member of the crew checked his own equipment for serviceability and all snags were carefully noted. We climbed, dived, banked and weaved; tested fuel tanks and pumps, radio, navigational and bombing equipment;

feathered and unfeathered propeller blades; swung turrets and guns; checked oxygen and intercom systems; checked pressures, temperatures, voltages, light switches, fuses and instruments – in fact, every effort was made to sort out anything which might give trouble on the night's trip.

On our return, I reported all snags to the sergeant and the tradesmen concerned, so that everything could be fixed in good time. The ground crew took a great interest in the aircraft and worked really hard to keep it serviceable. A tractor was hitched to 'William's' tail-wheel and he was turned round in dispersal, so that he faced the perimeter track. Almost before the wheels stopped rolling, a petrol bowser pulled across his nose and the long, snake-like hoses were hauled on to the wings and eager hands thrust Zwicky nozzles into the open petrol tanks. The dispersal point was a hive of activity and it was obvious that the ground crew were as excited about the trip as we were.

The crew-coach came along and we helped Doug and Eddie stow the guns on board, and then piled in after them. We toured the perimeter track, halting at several dispersal points to pick up crews who had been testing their aircraft. As usual, everybody talked at the same time and there was plenty of leg-pulling, but the conversation centred mainly on the forthcoming op and the possible target.

The bomb trolleys were already beginning to roll out to the aircraft and the boys nodded wisely on sighting the 4,000-pound 'cookies', 1,000-pound delayed-action bombs and the canisters of incendiaries. Sure to be another 'Ruhr bash' – especially as the fuel load was 1,250 gallons. Probably Duisburg, or Essen, or even Cologne again. Anyhow, why worry?

On arrival at the gun-cleaning room, we helped the gunners to carry the Brownings inside. The rest of us then took the flying-kit into the locker room, leaving Doug and Eddie to strip and clean the guns which would be returned to the aircraft during the afternoon. Reg Boys collected the helmets and disappeared into the Signals Section in order to test the mikes and headsets. Then when he had finished, I tested the oxygen masks for serviceability and checked them on the test-rig. Next, I sorted out my tool-kit, torches and spare equipment; examined my harness, Mae West, gloves, goggles and flying boots; then off to the Mess for lunch.

After lunch, Bill was busy in the Navigation Section getting his stuff ready for the trip, Corky was likewise occupied in the Bombing Section, Doug and Eddie had taken the guns out to the kite, the two

Reg's and I had the billet to ourselves. After writing a couple of letters, I decided to make my preparations and then try to snatch a short sleep before tea. After changing socks and underwear, I emptied my pockets and returned only the things which could safely be carried on an op. The list rarely varied – small wallet with treasured photographs, New Testament, two pencils, eraser and a folding-card, penknife, three handkerchiefs, cigarette case and lighter, and a small sum of money. I checked the identity discs and tiny silver horseshoe which I carried on a cord, necklace fashion. Next, I tested the security of the red bead-headed pin on the lapel of my blouse. This pin had become a treasured possession. At our first operational briefing, I 'lifted' it from the target map as we left the briefing room and stuck it into my lapel for luck. Such was the power of mascots and charms, that I would have been worried if I had to fly without it. The plated whistle which dangled from the hook on my battledress collar, was given a couple of trial blasts, bringing violent abuse from my snoozing companions. Finally, I slipped my 'escape knife' into the quick-release clip on my leather belt. With a contented sigh, I kicked off my shoes, loosened my collar and tie, and flopped down on the bed.

As I relaxed, my thoughts wandered to the folks at home and my heart was heavy. Not for them the thrill and interest of a bombing mission – the approach of evening would bring only worry and apprehension. The morning's radio news, with its 'Last night . . . in very great strength . . . forty-seven of our aircraft are missing,' would not ease the strain. The only relief, a letter in familiar handwriting, asking them not to worry as everything was going fine. I thought also of the girl who sent me such interesting letters. Dot was serving with the ATS as a spotter in a Heavy AA Battery and, being a great friend of my sister, I often met her whilst on leave. She was a grand type – the kind of girl I would like to marry, if I hadn't been a confirmed bachelor. Anyhow, operational flying and marriage just didn't mix, it wasn't fair to a girl. What future was there in being the wife of a man whose expectation of life was about twenty-four hours? Still, Dot meant more to me than I cared to admit. She had made 'Joe', the mascot, and sent him to look after the crew – if he did his stuff, there was no telling what might happen. Even confirmed bachelors had been known to change their minds!

I must have fallen to sleep at that point because the next thing I heard was the rattle of Bill's bicycle against the side of the hut, followed by the cry, 'Wakee! Wakee!' as our cheery little navigator breezed in through the open doorway. The other boys rolled in soon afterwards, so I sat up and fixed my collar and tie, resigning myself to the fact that further sleep would be impossible. We talked and smoked for a while and then strolled down to the Mess for a spot of tea before briefing.

There was an air of suppressed excitement about the briefing room and I felt that the serious business was really beginning. The skipper gave each member of the crew an escape-kit and we settled down in our chairs. I glanced at the gen-board on the wall, to make sure that 'William' was still serviceable and felt relieved when I saw 'BUNTEN – W' together with our times for take-off, set-course and time-on-target. I then jotted down on my folding-card the details applicable to my job. The room suddenly went quiet and everyone stood up as the Squadron Commander entered and took his place on the platform in front of the huge wall-map of Western Europe. We sat down again and the CO opened the briefing with the words, 'Gentlemen, your target for to-night is Cologne'. There was a buzz of excitement amongst the crews and Reg turned towards the rest of us and gave the thumbs-up sign.

The wall-map was then uncovered and we stared at the coloured strings and bead-pins indicating the route to and from the target. Rendezvous at Sheringham, in over the Dutch coast and out over the Belgian coast. Short trip – just how I liked them, excitement all the way, and no time to get bored or tired. Felt rather disappointed that it was Cologne again – had already been there twice. Was keen to have a crack at Essen, maybe have the chance next trip – if there was a next trip!

The CO gave us the broad outlines of the operation – about 750 aircraft, made up of Lancasters, Halifaxes, Stirlings and Wellingtons, were to attack at the times shown on the board; the 25 Lancasters of 103 Squadron would be in three phases, bombing from 20,000 feet or over; 'Oboe' Mosquitoes and Lancasters of the Pathfinder Force would mark the target with red TIs, backed up by green TIs; Main Force was to bomb reds or centre of the greens if reds not down; 'Wanganui' sky-marking would be used if conditions made it impossible for ground-marking to be seen; route as marked on map . . . As he unfolded the plan of campaign, I looked at the blackboard on which the Pathfinder technique to be used had been drawn in coloured chalk, and thought how pretty everything would look – from the air. I doubted whether the people of Cologne would share my views.

The CO was followed by the various specialists. The Met. man gave us the latest gen on the weather. Very comforting, too. Not much to worry about – clear for take-off, low temperatures at operating altitudes (grand for the engines but tough on the poor gunners), very little risk of icing anywhere on the trip, target expected to be clear by zero hour, slight risk of ground mist for return, no trouble from the moon. Intelligence reviewed past attacks on the city and gave us details of defences in the target area and at other points on the route. Positions of our convoys were given, with the timely warning to steer clear of them – naval types had been known to shoot first and ask questions after! As usual, he finished on a rather depressing note by advising us on the procedure to be taken in the event of our being unlucky enough to be shot down.

Whilst the Navigation Leader dealt in detail with the route, times and heights, I mentally calculated the amount of fuel we would use on the trip and estimated the order of using the tanks, so as to arrive over the target with approximately the same amount of petrol in each. The Bombing Leader ran through the various checks for the benefit of new crews and pleaded with the pilots to give their bomb aimers a chance by making a good run-up and holding the aircraft steady, after bombing, for a decent photo. Lots of other gen as well – there was more to bomb aiming than just picking out the aiming-point and pressing the bomb-tit.

Everybody paid great attention to the Gunnery Leader; his subject was of vital importance. By means of the map, he pointed out the danger spots on the route and the 'fighter boxes' through which we would pass; he warned against intruders at take-off and emphasised the risk of attack by fighters returning with the bomber stream. In view of the Met. forecast, gunners would have to be on the alert the whole time, taking extra care over the target area when aircraft would be silhouetted against the fires below. Most of us knew this stuff by heart but no crew could afford to be over-confident. Flying Control and Signals gave their information for the benefit of pilots and wireless ops and then the CO summarised the whole proceedings. He ended with a sincere, 'Good luck, chaps; and remember – twenty-five off on time, twenty-five aiming point photos, and twenty-five back!'

After the CO had left the briefing room, there was a rush to examine the target maps and route in greater detail. The air of excitement, so noticeable when I entered the room, had been replaced by a happier and more determined atmosphere. No need to ponder and argue now, we all knew the score. Slowly, the boys drifted from the room and the word 'Cologne' was tucked away into the back of each mind. The most important thing now was to get to grips with the operational meal.

After doing full justice to a four-course meal, I retired for my customary shave. There was always argument on the question of shaving immediately before an op. Some people thought that an unshaven face was less likely to be irritated by the oxygen mask, and that they felt tougher with a growth of beard. Turning over the problem in my mind as I plied brush and razor, I decided that shaving improved the morale. To feel fresh and clean was to feel confident and alert. Anyhow, it helped to fill in the time between the meal and final briefing – I hated to sit around twiddling my thumbs or pretending to read the daily papers.

As we strolled along to the locker room, I called at the armoury for the 'colours-of-the-day' cartridges. I was convinced that Reg Boys was the man to get them but I always fell for the job. He had the pleasure of 'pooping' them off, so why shouldn't he call for them? A few crews were already dressing when we arrived at the locker room and there was a lot of excited chatter, broken occasionally by loud threats and accusations from fellows who couldn't find their gloves or scarves. The smiling WAAFS were busy handing out parachutes and flying clothing, with a cheery word for everyone. Having retained our 'chutes after the morning's NFT, we went straight to the locker.

Bill found the key to the door, after searching through his pockets for several minutes, and we dumped our kit in little heaps on the concrete floor. Eddie and Doug had changed into long underwear at the billet and, as it was their practice to carry their kit to the aircraft and complete dressing just before take-off, they were soon ready. Reg, Bill and Reg Boys wore very little extra clothing, whilst Corky followed the gunners' example and always dressed at dispersal. The boys were amused at my slowness in changing but I believed in being fussy – I hated to feel chafed or uncomfortable on a trip, and felt that a few extra minutes in the locker room were amply repaid by the consequent freedom from irritation.

After removing my shoes, collar and tie, I donned my normal ops wear: battledress; silk scarf; white sweater; long stockings; and flying boots. The chamois gloves went into my trousers pocket, then I wrapped harness, 'chute and helmet inside the Mae West. With this bundle and the log-board in one hand, and toolbag in the other, I made my way to the crew room for the final briefing.

The crew room was packed with men and equipment, and there was a real 'fug' from the cigarettes and pipes; navigators were working on the large, square table and the other categories were filling in their particular forms and log-sheets. Final briefing was quite informal. The CO and specialists gave us the latest gen, received since the main briefing, and a few last-minute alterations. Watches were then synchronised, the Nav. Leader calling the time, and the briefing ended when the CO had satisfied himself that everyone fully understood the various aspects of the night's operation. Crews began to leave and I nipped smartly into the MO's room, next door, for a few squirts from the nose-spray and to collect our caffeine tablets (known as 'wakee-wakee tablets' because of their peculiar properties of warding off sleep).

Outside the crew room, the coaches were waiting to take us to the aircraft. We made our way to the 'C' Flight coach and climbed on board, checking our stuff as we did so – flying clothing and 'chutes, Bill's navigation bag and sextant, the carrier-pigeon in its little yellow box and the ration box. The latter contained flasks of coffee, chocolate, barley-sugar sweets, tins of orange juice and packets of chewing gum. The crews of Bob Cant and Van Rolleghen climbed in and the coach pulled away to the accompaniment of 'Cheerios' and thumbs-up signs from the other crews.

After a few minutes, we swung into the dispersal point of 'U-Uncle' and Bob and his boys collected their kit and jumped out. We wished them 'All the best' and boasted that we would be snug in bed before they had touched-down with their dilapidated old crate. 'Van's' crew left at 'Z-Zebra' and we carried on to 'William'. I thought what grand types they all were; laughing, talking and leg-pulling, they were representative of all that was best in the world's manhood. In six or seven hours' time, we would be with them again, arguing and swapping experiences of the night's trip – we hoped!

The ground crew gave us a hand with our equipment and assured us that everything was ready for the preliminary run-up. I made my outside checks, giving a slight shudder as I noted how poor 'William' seemed to sag under his heavy load. Hated to see tyres bulging and oleo-legs riding low – even though it was quite normal with an all-up-weight of 63,000 pounds. Climbing inside, I made my way up to the cockpit, checking as I went. Reg and I started the engines and, after warming-up, gave each a thorough check at the various throttle openings. During the run-up, each crew member tested his own equipment – everything was 'bang on'. I stopped the engines and the boys tumbled outside for a smoke and a game of cards, leaving me to re-check and prepare for the trip. I looked up at 'Joe' and gave him a friendly pat on the shoulder – he, also, had a busy night before him.

Later, I joined the boys and smoked a cigarette. All was quiet until Chesterton, in 'Sugar', and Van, in 'Zebra', started their engines; Reg glanced at his watch and said it was time we got weaving. The gunners struggled into their electrical clothing and bulky flying suits, and pulled on layers of gloves – watched by an interested crowd of local villagers, standing on the main road just outside the 'drome. The ground crew wished us luck and we moved up to our crew-stations. At a nod from Reg, I pressed the starter buttons and, one by one, the four Merlins roared into life. A crew-check over the intercom, confirmation from Doug that the rear door was closed, a final look round as the brakes were released, and 'William' began to roll slowly forward.

Even before we poked our nose out of dispersal, I spotted the Flight Commander's van hurtling round the perimeter track. It stopped on our starboard side and a hand, giving a vigorous thumbs-down sign, was pushed out of the sidescreen. Reg braked to a standstill and, at that moment, two yellow Very lights from the control tower snaked up into the evening sky. A stream of oaths sizzled over the intercom – Bill flung his maps and charts on to the floor – and I snapped up the engine cut-off switches. Of all the confounded luck! A last-minute 'scrub'! Twelve hours of working, planning, wondering, waiting – and all for nothing.

That night, the citizens of Cologne slept peacefully in their beds.

The Sergeants' Mess at Elsham could hardly have been described as palatial, but the social atmosphere and squadron spirit was terrific. The boys of '103' who crowded into the building transformed it into a home – a gay, exciting home. Sprawling in cane-bottomed chairs or pacing the well-worn carpets, they breathed life and adventure into every brick and slab of concrete. The Ante Room, when empty, was almost bleak but when full it was the cosiest, friendliest place imaginable. Every chair occupied; card-tables surrounded by 'brag' and 'poker' fiends; energetic types knocking lumps out of the table-tennis table; the stock tunes, 'You are my Sunshine' and 'Maybe', oozing from the radiogram; the piano dancing under the ministrations of Chesterton's wireless operator; the ever-smiling steward handing out drinks from the pigeon-hole bar; and, above all, the incessant talk, laughter and good comradeship.

The radio news-bulletins always had good audiences, the six Greenwich 'pips' were the only things which could ever silence the Ante Room. The report of the previous night's raid and the number of missing aircraft was, of course, the main item of interest. Usually, the RAF lost anything from thirty to fifty aircraft, and we had to admit that Bomber Command was taking a hammering as well as giving one. Apart from the news, the most outstanding broadcast was a recording made by a BBC reporter – Wynford Vaughan Thomas – who took part in a raid on Berlin. This was really good and gave a faithful impression of a successful trip in a Lanc. Excitement was added by the shooting down of a fighter over the target. This incident was received with loud groans and shouts of 'Line!' from the boys, and was treated as just a piece of 'window dressing' for the benefit of the public.

Accommodation in the dining-hall was also inadequate and it was necessary to have two or three 'sittings' at meal times. This, however, did not affect the quality or the quantity of the food. Napoleon, so history relates, maintained that an army marches on its stomach; he would have been favourably impressed by the catering at Elsham. Annoying as the 'sittings' business certainly was, it had its advantages. Each crew, as far as possible, dined at a separate table but, due to the overcrowding, no table was every empty and we were not reminded by the sight of unoccupied chairs that two or three crews had failed to return from the previous night's raid. Whilst having every sympathy for our unfortunate colleagues, we tried to forget their loss as soon as possible. Not that crews were ever really forgotten but rather that they were mentally put on one side.

On non-flying days, lectures were sometimes laid on for the squadron and I always found them very interesting. On occasion, chaps who had escaped after being shot down over enemy territory lectured on their experiences and gave advice on outwitting the Hun on the deck. Van Rolleghen gave us a racy account of his adventures after the fall of Belgium, when he eluded the enemy and made his way to Britain to continue the fight in the Royal Air Force.

One day, we were honoured by a visit from the Commander-in-Chief, Bomber Command. Air Chief Marshal Sir Arthur Harris was given a terrific cheer as he walked on to the platform in the station cinema. 'Butch' – as we called him – wasted no time on formalities and said that he had come to listen to what we had to say. He invited suggestions, criticisms and opinions – nothing barred – on anything which we considered might improve the aircraft, squadron or command. As question after question was fired across the room, I studied the man who had earned the title of 'The Hammer of the Reich'. He looked older and kinder than I had imagined, but there was no doubt that he had a cool, calculating brain, and his whole bearing suggested that he would be utterly ruthless when occasion demanded. It was obvious that he was proud of his men and aircraft, and he promised us an extremely busy time in the coming months. The man-to-man talking revealed the fact that he was no mere figure-head, content to sit at HQ and pull strings, but that he knew most of the answers and could slug it out with the boys in a manner which proved he valued an honest opinion, be it expressed by Group Captain or Sergeant. I felt that his one ambition was to batter the enemy into an early submission and that he believed Bomber Command, given a free hand, was powerful enough to do it.

The crew had settled down comfortably in the once-despised Nissen hut and we spent many happy hours within its corrugated walls. We discussed every possible subject and often had some fierce arguments – always taken in good part, with no danger of frayed tempers. Corky, Bill and Reg Boys were very often writing to their respective lady-loves. They were definitely the keen types in the crew. I was more erratic, preferring to write when I felt in the mood, rather than commit myself to a timetable. Mail played a very important part in our lives in those days and the RAF, fully realising the fact, made every effort to ensure that the postal service was as efficient as possible. Every station had its own Post Office, staffed by trained personnel and run on 'Civvy Street' lines.

My mail, at that particular time, brought me happiness, amusement and sadness. In the first instance, the confirmed bachelor had fallen under the age-old spell during a previous leave and, in several pages of soul-stirring pleading, I had asked Dot to marry me. In a positive dither of excitement, I awaited the reply and finally the precious letter arrived – I was accepted! We were to be married as soon as I got my 'screening' leave at the end of the tour. It therefore became impera-tive that I complete my tour in one piece; obviously, I couldn't let the dear girl down.

News from 'Grindlestone' Green was always good. He had made a grand recovery after his accident and, although encased in plaster from neck to hips, he was able to walk again. Already, he was planning for the future and even suggested that he might be able to 'flannel' his way into a job as glider pilot! I could not help but admire his pluck and keenness, and compare it with the attitude of some men who pleaded every ailment imaginable in order to wangle an 'honourable' discharge. The enthusiastic references to pretty nurses showed that Jimmy's outlook on life was rapidly returning to normal. He took a dim view of my decision to desert the ranks of happy bachelors but grudgingly admitted that I was a very lucky man. Against his better nature and judgment, he promised to act as best man on the great day.

I was greatly amused by a paragraph in a letter from my sister, Marion. She related an incident in which she mentioned to a friend

Jack Osborne, reported missing after the raid on Mulheim on the night of 22/23 June 1943

that I had completed several operations, having thirty to do in all. The friend was extremely sympathetic and hoped that I would soon recover from the operations and be safely invalided home!

Another letter brought the dread news that Jack Osborne was reported missing from the raid on Mulheim, on the night of 22/23 June 1943. This was his third mission from Holme-on-Spalding Moor and Ludford Magna, having previously been on the Wuppertal and Krefeld efforts with 101 Squadron. I thought sadly of all the glorious plans we had made at St Athan. Jack had the bad luck to be delayed at Lindholme by illness and then, so soon after finally getting on to an operational squadron, had failed to return. Fate had struck a savage and early blow.

As the battering of the Ruhr continued throughout the early summer, it became increasingly obvious that, with the approach of longer periods of darkness, Bomber Command would soon be seeking pastures new. There had been rumours and counter-rumours of long-range trips, eyes were wont to wander farther east on the target maps, there was the odd occasion when fuel tanks had actually been filled to capacity, and there had been a few early scrubs. The tension, which had been building up for days, was broken when the CO informed us at briefing that the German capital was at last to feel the full weight of an attack in strength by Bomber Command. A spontaneous burst of cheering greeted this announcement.

We had all wanted a 'bash' at the 'Big City' more than anything else in the world and this was it, for 'William' and crew. There was quite a crowd of onlookers at the end of the runway and, as Reg swung 'William' into position, I gave a quick acknowledgment of their hand-waves and thumbs-up signs. Good old 'Doc' Henderson was there, as usual, and certain of the crews who were not operating had come along to give us a cheer. A number of ground staff lads and WAAFs had also turned up and it felt comforting to know that we had their prayers and best wishes. In the same quick glance, I noticed the fire-tender and the 'blood-waggon' standing by, and hoped that their services would not be required, either before or after the trip.

'William' rocked slightly as Reg applied the brakes, and the skipper and I re-checked every control and setting. The previous aircraft was just getting airborne when we got our 'green' from the checkered caravan and Reg, dead cool as usual, murmured, 'OK chaps, here we go!'. The engine note increased to a roar and, as the brakes were released, 'William' rolled slowly forward, gathering speed as the throttles were progressively opened. A quick check on the engine instruments and exhaust flames, and then I pushed the throttle-levers through the 'gate' and nipped-on the friction-nut. I smiled at Reg and reported, 'All engines OK, full power on!'. The aircraft tore down the runway like a thing possessed, with the four Merlins screaming out their war-song. Reg gave me, 'Wheels up!' as he eased 'William' off the deck and, pressing back the safety-catch with my wrist, I whipped up the undercart-lever. After our gallant aircraft had tucked his legs into their nacelles, I reduced power and raised the flaps by degrees. Mother Earth began to slip away into the evening dusk and, as we entered the cloud-layer which was blanketing the setting sun, I felt that she would retire gracefully to light her lamps against our return.

Climbing through cloud, we gained height over base, each one of us busy at his own job. Corky was stuffing propaganda leaflets into the bomb-compartment – they would be delivered, along with the bombs, on Jerry's doorstep. Reg and I were getting 'William' settled into his stride for the long trip. Bill had drawn his black-out curtain across and was busy passing out times, courses and speeds – and searching for his spare pencils! Reg Boys, in his own little world of switches, knobs and dials, was already beginning to perspire and craftily turned down the heating-system at his side, knowing full well that Corky would soon be calling for more heat! Eddie and Doug were swinging the turrets and accustoming their eyes to the evening light, at the same time keeping a look-out for the presence of other aircraft – with their trigger-fingers ready to deal with any intruding night fighters. 'Joe', the mascot, stood cool and confident; defying the powers-of-evil to do their worst.

We broke cloud into the glory of a late summer evening. A few scattered tufts of medium cloud picked up the rays of the reluctantly-setting sun and tossed them to us in an assortment of reds, golds and violets. The sky, blood-red where the sun blazed angrily on the devouring horizon, was mellowing from its familiar azure to a darker blue in which the first stars had already begun to twinkle. It was a beautiful and impressive sight and, as I gazed, I assured myself that if it was true – as aircrew alleged – that 'Only birds and fools fly – and birds don't fly at night!' then I was thrice-content to be a fool.

And as I mused, I watched the other aircraft. They were all around us; above, below and on all sides; some, mere specks in the distance, others near enough for their squadron letters to be distinguished; their grim, black shapes relieved only by the red and green naviga-tion lights and blue exhaust-flames, and occasionally by a momentary flicker of light as the sun's rays caught the perspex canopies. But pleasant as the scene outside my window was proving, there were sterner things to occupy my mind and time. After a check on the altimeter, I turned on the oxygen and warned the crew to connect their masks, check the supply and report back. On re-checking the operation of the fuel tank selector-cocks, I found to my surprise that the starboard cock had jammed. Fortunately, the snag was soon sorted out. I detached the panels from the inside of the fuselage wall to check the run of the chains, and spotted a short strip of metal wedged between the sprocket and the chain. Somewhat relieved by the simple solution, I removed the culprit and made a mental note to have a few quiet words with the ground crew. My log-sheet was already recording the fact that 'William' was in grand form and it was with a smile of satisfaction that I heard Bill tell Reg that we were over base at our briefed altitude and could now set course. Reg repeated the bearing and turned 'William' into the darkening east – that east which held so much hatred and hostility but, for us, no terrors.

We crossed the home-coast, over our rendezvous point, at 16,000 feet. 'George', the automatic pilot, had taken over from Reg and was climbing 'William' up to our operational height of 22,000 feet. I had changed the superchargers into 'S' gear and, as the engines were behaving perfectly, I assisted the gunners by keeping a good look-out for other aircraft – friendly or otherwise. Although the sky in the west was not yet completely dark, the assassin's cloak was slowly being drawn over our shoulders. The luminous dials on the instrument panels were already coming to life, looking like little groups of glow-worms sitting round in circles. High in the heavens, our old friend the 'Plough' was plainly visible. I was always happy to see it and automatically murmured my old catch-phrase, 'Port side, going out; starboard side, coming home'.

It was still possible to see some of the other Lancs; a few were foolishly burning their navigation lights, several high-flying types were leaving vapour trails behind them, exhaust-glow gave away the position of others, and one was keeping very close company with us. Once or twice it had drifted across our roof in that curious, apparent, sideways motion and Eddie voiced his feelings on the matter in a few well-chosen words. A collision, just as we were getting settled down, would have been very annoying and, in any case, the North Sea was certain to be jolly cold at night.

Reg made a crew check and, apart from the usual minor snags, everything was 'bang on'. Bill complained that his 'Gee' set was not too good but he was 'coping'; Doug's warning-light had flashed on a few times and he had effected a temporary cure by covering the glass with a wad of chewing gum; Eddie had the usual moan about his attention being distracted by the insulator on Reg Boys' aerial; whilst our worthy bomb aimer was calling for more heat. It was good to hear their voices. We had a quiet crew but when they spoke over the intercom, I felt the warmth of their friendship. Battle orders would prove that there were several hundred aircraft proceeding towards Germany at that precise moment but, nevertheless, we seven were alone. Each man responsible for his own task and each prepared to sacrifice everything for the well-being of the crew as a whole.

We were at 20,000 feet when I first noticed the faint pencils of light prodding the dark sky many miles ahead. As we flew nearer, the faint lights sharpened into the cold, blue-white beams of searchlights – some playing a lone hand and others in criss-crossing groups. As if realising that there was fun to be had for the asking, the flak-ships and land-batteries bestirred themselves, and soon the curving strings of 'flaming onions' and the dull-red flashes of bursting heavy flak lent colour and interest to the proceedings. Then one searchlight fastened on to a tiny, glittering object and immediately, a score of beams hurried over to lend a hand. The dreaded 'cone' was quickly formed and flak began to pump up its centre to the silvery target at the apex. The cone leaned over from side to side in an endeavour to hold its prey and, suddenly, the silver object changed into a golden ball of fire which slowly began to slide down the exultant beams. One of our aircraft was already missing and the gunners down below on Texel Island chalked up their first success of the night. The enemy's front gate had been kicked open but our entry would be hotly disputed.

'Enemy coast coming up, navigator,' said Corky. A rather obvious remark to make, as far as we in the cockpit were concerned, but to Bill, behind his black-out curtains, it provided a rough check on his navigation and time. I sensed a spirit of high adventure as I repeated Corky's words to myself, 'Enemy coast coming up!'. What man, with British blood in his veins, could resist the thrill of pride and sense of achievement I felt as we roared steadily towards the outer bastions of that forbidden territory into which – so boasted the swashbuckling Goering – no RAF aircraft would ever penetrate. I could be forgiven for comparing our crew with the men of Agincourt, '. . . We few, we happy few, we band of brothers . . .', and feel with them that,

'. . . gentlemen in England now abed
Shall think themselves accursed they were not here,
And hold their manhoods cheap while any speaks
That fought with us . . .'

At 22,000 feet, we levelled out and, having evaded the inquisitive searchlights, settled down to a steady cruise to the next turning point. A Lanc. on our starboard bow was doing a spot of weaving but we stooged along straight-and-level, in 'George', as was our usual practice. I looked back through the perspex blister and saw the gun-turrets swinging; Eddie and Doug were still busy searching the sky. We could expect fighters at any time and it was not advisable to be beaten to the draw. Textbooks praised the rate-of-fire and bullet-pattern of the .303 turrets but there was no denying that a Lanc., at the receiving end of a burst of cannon-shell, was a very dead duck.

Air defences over Cologne

37

Away to starboard, I could see a running battle taking place. Both aircraft were invisible but the streaks of tracer told their own story. The end came very quickly. A dull-red ball appeared in the sky and, growing bigger and brighter every second, slowly began to lose height. As it fell, sporadic bursts of tracer came from the rear of the flames, obviously the Lanc. had lost the battle and the fighter would be hurrying away to find fresh customers. The raging inferno broke into two parts and, several thousand feet below, was temporarily hidden by a thickish layer of cloud. We were now leaving the falling aircraft behind but I saw the glow reappear beneath the cloud and then a vicious glare, like the sudden opening of a furnace door, tore a ragged gash in the darkness. That, I well knew, was the Lanc. hitting the deck. The 'chopper' was already beginning to swing.

'William' was steadily eating up the route to the target and everything was going fine. The engines were in magnificent form and the entries of instrument readings on my log-sheet began to look monotonous. Thanks to Bill, we were bang on track and dead on time. A few of the other aircraft were not quite so lucky; they had strayed away to starboard and had been given a hot reception by Osnabrück. The searchlight and flak people were really annoyed at the intrusion and were teaching the off-track types a sharp lesson. I did not actually see any aircraft shot down but the accuracy of the shooting, for height, pointed to the possibility of damaged wings and fuel tanks. There had also been a real firework display over on the port side which we found comfortably exciting – comfortable because we were miles away at the time, and exciting because of the fantastic amount of light flak that was being pumped up. A 'dummy' attack had been laid on Bremen and the defenders were banging away with everything that would fire. The whole area was brilliantly confused, with the orange trails of light flak tracer intricately weaving through the forest of searchlight beams – it seemed impossible for anything to penetrate but the occasional dull-red flashes at deck-level proved that there was nothing 'dummy' about the bombs which were being dropped. Nice work, boys! Probably have drawn some of the fighters away from the main attack.

As we approached the last turning-point, a carpet of medium cloud began to roll slowly over the countryside and, one by one, the twinkling lights on the ground were hidden from view. The Met. people had forecast the probability of a cloud-covered target and, rather resentfully, we realised that the attack would develop into a 'Wanganui' sky-marking effort. There was a sense of frustration in the 'blind' attacks and one always had the uncomfortable feeling that the bombs were hitting everything except the target. Still, it had its advantages – searchlights were comparatively ineffective and flak was not so great a menace and, providing the cloud tops were high enough, fighters could be avoided by utilising cloud-cover. Thus did an impartial Nature protect both friend and foe.

South-east of Berlin, Reg swung 'William' on to course for the run-in to the target and, after a quick crew-check, warned us to keep a good look-out for fighters or other aircraft. Corky was busy pushing out 'Window' and making final adjustments to his bomb-sight and computer-box; Reg had taken over from 'George' so that the compressor could feed the bombing equipment; I made a thorough check of all control settings and switches, and increased the oxygen supply, ready for the extra altitude we hoped to gain after bombing; Bill juggled with times and distances; Reg Boys left his sets, to search from the astrodrome; and the ever-watchful Doug and Eddie continued to scour the night sky.

The dark carpet beneath us began to change to a patchy white as searchlights were trained on to its underside; and bombers, hitherto unseen, came into view as their black shapes were sharply silhouetted against the light background. Bursts of heavy flak peppered the sky, obviously box-barrage stuff, OK for height but not so accurate as the predicted variety – 'Window' was proving its worth once again. Away in the distance, the first flares went down and the familiar vivid red glare, with green stars dripping from the centre, told us that the Pathfinder boys had confirmed the Met. forecast; the cloud was too thick for ground-markers to be seen. Without warning, a brilliant yellow-white glare lit up the sky on our port bow – then another, to starboard – one more to port, further ahead – another to starboard – and then, at intervals, right on to the target! We soon realised what the score was – the crafty Hun was laying illuminating flares right along our track, providing a brightly-lit street down which his night fighters could patrol, making contacts at leisure.

Almost before the gunners had accustomed their eyes to the new conditions, Jerry began to reap dividends from his ingenuity. Doug reported an Me 109 moving in and Reg prepared to take evasive action. I looked back through my starboard blister and saw the enemy fighter, fairly high on our starboard quarter. There was a Lanc. stooging off our starboard wing-tip and Reg pulled away slightly so that we could have more sky to play about in. Over the intercom., I could hear Doug inviting the swine to come in closer and threatening to blast him to hell. At that moment, the fighter dived in to the attack and turned in towards the other Lanc. with its cannons blazing. There was a blinding flash as the shells struck home and the bomber became a raging inferno which, in its agony, coughed out a dazzling array of greens, reds and yellows. In an incredibly short time, an angry cloud of black smoke was the only visible reminder that another Lancaster, with its crew of seven, had flown its last mission.

Away in front, the clouds gradually became saturated with red from the fires below, like the slow spreading of a stain on a white sheet. The sky-markers were still going down and the fighter-flares still hung in the sky, and the general effect was as though we were riding down Blackpool promenade during 'Illuminations' week – although the occasion was not quite so peaceful. The illusion was quickly shattered when Corky quietly murmured, 'Bomb doors open!' and we commenced our bombing run. Straight and level, we flew steadily on, more vulnerable than at any other period of the trip, and with every second seeming like an hour. A Lanc. drifted across our canopy and I could see its yawning bomb-bay, not more than twenty feet above us – much too near for comfort. We ran up on the flares and, at last, Corky pressed the 'tit' and our messengers of high explosives and incendiaries swept down to fulfil their destiny. I was too busy watching the kite overhead to notice the shudder as 'William' disgorged his load and then, with a sigh of relief, I saw their bombs come showering down past our starboard wing-tip. We had been hit by a falling bomb on a previous trip – luckily without serious damage – and I just hated to think of the beastly things coming through the roof.

Corky asked for the bomb doors to be closed, Reg held steady for the camera, and then turned on to the course out of the target. It was all over. Our long-cherished hopes of blitzing Berlin were realised at last – but we all wished the weather conditions had been better.

The 'Reaper' was still busy on the run out to the coast and we saw three more aircraft go down in flames. Then I jumped for joy when I saw a single-engined fighter hurtling down at terrific speed in a practically vertical descent, with grey-black smoke streaming behind like a comet's tail. It was good to know that the battle was not going all one way. We kept our height until we reached the enemy coast and then began to let-down for a fast run home. The engines were grand and we had bags of petrol, so we were not faced with a possible ditching or a landing at an emergency 'drome – unlike some of the poor devils who would be preparing to touch down on the watery runways of the North Sea. The Air/Sea Rescue boats would, at that very moment, be speeding out to save the lives of 'press-on' types who preferred the danger and hardship of a night-ditching to the somewhat safer course of baling out and risking capture on land.

At 8,000 feet, I removed my oxygen mask with a feeling of relief and brought out the coffee flask. For seven hours I had been chewing gum and I was as dry as dust. I was to remain as dry as dust – my flask was broken and, to my disgust, I found that the coffee in the other flasks had gone sour.

Soon, the welcoming searchlights on the home coast came into view and we knew that we were amongst friends again. Several frisky types were pooping-off 'colours-of-the-day' cartridges and a few aircraft were burning navigation lights. The blackness of the night was slowly being pushed back by the rather hesitant dawn which peeped carefully over the eastern horizon. With the gradually increasing light, the red glow of the exhaust-stubs was dying away and black numerals and fingers superseded the glow-worms on the instrument panels. As we crossed the coast, dotted circles of light on the ground, with the attendant 'Sandra' lights, indicated the positions of airfields, and we knew that – true to her promise – Mother Earth had placed her lights in the window to guide and welcome our return.

At last, we sighted Elsham. Reg took over from 'George' and then called up Flying Control. Five crews had previously called up but they must have got down pretty smartly for we were given 'Prepare to land' as we stooged across the 'drome. We swung into the circuit and made our preparations. Corky came up from the nose and stood behind my position; Bill gathered his charts and maps and stuffed them into his bag, ready for a quick getaway after landing; Reg Boys passed the Aldis lamp forward so that I could use it whilst taxiing; and Reg and I checked all our control-settings and clipped on our masks. With wheels safely down and locked, and flaps partially down, we turned into the 'funnel' at 700 feet and made our approach. Nicely 'in the green' and lined-up beautifully on the runway, with flaps fully down, I cut the throttles back as we wafted over the boundary and 'William' sank on to the tarmac with scarcely a shudder. Reg had brought us in to his usual wizard landing. As we rolled along the runway, I opened my window and breathed a contented sigh as the good, clean air of England swept into my face.

The ground crew signalled us into dispersal with their torches and, after testing the magnetos and clearing the engines, I snapped off the cut-off switches. The four 'Merlins' slowed and gradually stopped –

each having completed about one-and-a-quarter million revs during the trip. The boys bustled out of the aircraft with their piles of kit and, before I followed, I paused for a moment to give 'Joe' a thankful pat on the shoulder, the gallant little man had done the trick again. The ground crew welcomed us as we climbed out and asked about 'William'. I assured them that he was absolutely 'bang on' and getting better every trip.

How good it was to feel the ground under my feet once more. And how glorious that first puff of the priceless cigarette. The workaday world may count its treasures in precious metals and stones, but for honest worth, give me the sensation of *terra firma* and tobacco, after eight hours flying.

A few minutes later, the crew-coach pulled alongside and we were whisked off to the locker room to change and then down to 'Ops' for debriefing. As we walked along, aircraft were still droning around the circuit and I wondered if all our kites had made the grade.

The Ops room was crowded when we arrived. Returned crews were laughing and discussing the trip in abnormally loud voices – loud because the sound of the engines would still be roaring in their ears. The crews looked dirty and tired but there was, about them all, an air of pride in a job well done. WAAFS were handing out cups of extra-sweet tea, well-laced with rum to chase away fatigue and to replace some of our lost energy; the padre handed out cigarettes and chatted with the boys; and the section leaders received reports and log-sheets from the various categories. From time to time, everyone glanced at the gen-board on which the names of crews were added as they reported back from the trip. The list was lengthening but there was some uneasiness about two or three of the 'early' crews who ought to have been back – possibly they had been delayed by engine-trouble or had been forced to land away from base. At intervals, crews left for debriefing and soon it was our turn. With infinite patience, the debriefing officer drew from us the story of our part in the night's attack. We all felt very tired and found it hard to concentrate. Recounting the incidents seemed an effort – like the hazy recalling of a half-forgotten film.

After debriefing, we went over to the Mess for breakfast and, having done justice to a really good meal, finally made our way to the billet. The sky was quite light and the sun was already thrusting out its first rays; birds were arguing amongst themselves in the tree-tops; and early-rising farm folk were leisurely making their way to the fields. All was peaceful and normal. As I looked around, I found it hard to believe that only a few hours ago we had been over the 'Big City'.

How glorious to climb between the sheets! I never sat down on a trip and my legs had been taking the strain since the operational meal on the previous day. I felt so weary that I fell to sleep as soon as I laid my head on the pillow.

Early in the afternoon, we awakened and – feeling fully rested – pottered along to the Mess for a late lunch. As we entered the Ante Room, the BBC announcer was saying, 'Last night, aircraft of Bomber Command attacked Berlin in great strength. Forty-nine of our aircraft are missing'.

During the early years of the war, it had been the policy of Bomber Command to lay on attacks when the moon was full but, in 1943, this was found to be tantamount to suicide. Originally, the idea was to utilise the light of the moon for the easier identification of targets. With the introduction of new radar aids, coupled with the success of the Pathfinder Force, and the ever-increasing menace of night fighters, it was realised that the moon had become a deadly enemy. Thus it was that, after a busy period of operating, we looked forward to the 'moon stand-down'; this was the time for Mess dances, parties and a general relaxation. It was also the time for increased training. Flight Commanders seized the opportunity to get the boys airborne on bombing practice, fighter affiliation, air-to-sea firing and formation flying; the link-trainer was kept very busy and the Gunnery Leader dusted off his guns and traps, and sent his section out to do some clay-pigeon shooting.

I always enjoyed the flying training. We had fun and there was always the excuse for indulging in a little unofficial dicing. On bombing practice, Doug would pull Corky's leg by pretending that he had seen our last bomb make a direct hit on a farmhouse, or that a car was blazing on the main road as a result of Corky's attempts to hit the practice target! The air/sea firing was carried out over the North Sea, east of Mablethorpe. Reg Boys would drop a sea-marker, which left a large patch of aluminium powder floating on the water, and the gunners would bang away at this as Reg flew over at varying heights and attitudes. After the gunners had fired off their ammo. Reg would bring 'William' down to within a few feet of the waves and whistle him along like a speedboat. Fighter-affil. was always a thrill and Reg threw 'William' around the sky in an attempt to shake off the 'attacking' Spitfires. During these manoeuvres, the effects of 'G', both positive and negative, were very pronounced – it was very amusing to see small articles falling upwards during a sudden dive and to experience the inability to rise from one's seat in a very steep climb. Formation flying often gave us the excuse to pay visits to the home towns of the boys. The drill was to do a few circuits in the selected district and waggle the wings; invariably, a proud mother or wife would appear in the garden below and acknowledge the visit by waving a tablecloth or towel. Having said 'Hello', we made for our pre-arranged rendezvous where we formated on the other aircraft (who had also been visiting) and flew back to base on completion of the 'exercise'. Another feature of our training was that it was usually carried out to the accompaniment of dance music, carefully selected and relayed over the intercom by Reg Boys; our version of 'Music while you work'.

Training was not all fun, of course; many good crews were killed and many valuable aircraft destroyed on the simplest of exercises. At Elsham, we had a pilot who was notorious for his 'split turns' off the deck, and the more experienced chaps prophesied early disaster if he persisted in taking risks. Inevitably, came the day when news reached the squadron that he had crashed on take-off. As the crash took place at a nearby 'drome, we didn't get the full story but the general comment was, 'I told you so!' Another of our kites was taking off on an exercise when a terrific swing to port sent it tearing across the grass at the side of the runway. It tore through a hedge, crossed the main road, rocked over a ditch – where the undercart collapsed – and finally crashed on to its belly, with its nose over-hanging the famous Elsham quarry. Flames enveloped the aircraft as it came to rest and we onlookers felt very relieved when we saw the crew come tumbling out of the escape-hatches and scramble to safety. They were lucky to get away with it. The fire-tender had consider-able difficulty in negotiating the ditch and the kite was practically a total wreck by the time the flames were subdued. Out on a training trip, one morning, we saw a Halifax flying rather low on three engines; without the slightest warning, it turned on to its side and went straight into the deck. Beyond circling the spot and reporting the matter to base, there was nothing we could do to help. These, and similar, crashes made me realise that there might be some truth in the old saying, 'An aeroplane – despite its apparent virtues – is out to kill, from the moment it becomes airborne'.

With the passage of time, promotion came to certain members of the crew; Reg got his WO, Bill, Eddie and Reg Boys became Flight

Sergeants. There was a sort of gentleman's agreement between us that we would remain NCOs until the end of the tour, so that we could all live in the same quarters and use the same Mess – a very big factor in maintaining crew spirit and co-operation.

It was now possible for flight engineers to obtain commissions and, in consequence, the Flight Engineer Leader came into being, bringing us in line with the other categories. 'Jock' Brehenny was the first commissioned engineer on the squadron and he became our section leader – at last, we engineers had a room of our own and things began to get organised. I considered the question of applying for a commission after I was screened from ops but decided that planning my forthcoming marriage would occupy my mind for the time being. In addition, I had formed the opinion that there was no financial advantage in becoming an officer – a rather important point to a man who was about to take unto himself a wife.

The Mess became a real home-from-home as the 'older' crews were screened and the crews with whom we were more familiar assumed the mantle of experience and dignity. It was then our turn to welcome new crews to the squadron and relate to them the stirring adventures of the past, pausing occasionally to point out such famous crews as Stoneman's, Chesterton's, Breckon's, Cant's, Drew's, Egan's, Steele's, Van Rolleghen's and, of course, Bunten's! The famous footprints on the Ante Room ceiling were pointed to with pride, almost as though we had been personally responsible for their presence. It was our privilege, too, to claim acquaintance with the chap who could chew razor-blades and beer glasses – an accomplishment possessed only by the few. To see him drink a beer and then eat the glass, was an unforgettable experience.

The food continued to improve and – with the addition of oranges, chocolate, sweets, Horlicks tablets, orange juice, cake and biscuits from the Naafi stores; our flying rations and issue of 'pep' tablets and capsules – we were almost as well-fed as the American troops! In the event of our needing anything extra, we could always repair to the Church Army canteen on the station, where we were able to have a chat with our ground crew over a cup of 'char'. Our boys were good types and we liked them to know that we really did appreciate their work on the aircraft.

We operational types were fortunate in getting leave frequently and regularly. Every seventh week, we could be seen hurrying down to Barnetby railway station or thumbing lifts to Doncaster, all set for six days of freedom. A welcome feature of the morning-of-leave pay parade was the extra five-bob-a-day 'good time' money, thought-fully provided – so rumour had it – by Lord Nuffield, to mark his appreciation of the work done by the Bomber Boys.

On one of my leaves, Dot and I arranged to meet Bill and his wife in Manchester. We did a show and, after tea, went along to Belle Vue Speedway, where we were joined by the one-and-only 'Grindlestone' Green. Jimmy was in splendid form and looked quite fit. Apart from a tendency to tire easily, he pronounced himself ready to return to duty. The medical people, however, had other views and insisted on a period of convalescence. We all enjoyed the speedway meeting and thrilled to the roar of highly-tuned engines, the reek of doped fuels, and the keen racing.

There had been no further news of Jack Osborne when I visited his folks, and I was forced to adopt an optimistic attitude for their sakes. My one remaining hope, however, was that he had managed to contact the underground movement in the Low Countries and was lying low until it was considered safe to make an attempt to reach England. There had been many instances of evaders taking months to return to this country, and I had no doubts about Jack's ability to make the grade if he was still alive.

It was about this time that Dot laid claim to fuller recognition as an active participant in the air war. She had been on duty, as a spotter, on the night when her battery 'bagged' an Me 410 with a direct hit – the first '410' to be shot down over this country. One of the aircraft propeller-blades had been salvaged and was later presented to the battery as a war trophy. I assured her that, in future, 'William' and crew would take great care to avoid flying in the vicinity of Mitcham, Surrey. The success might have made the '499' gunners 'trigger-happy' and we had no wish to join the ranks of those who had been shot down by friendly guns.

The crew and I went into Grimsby, one day, and met some of Reg Burton's boys. The last time we saw them was when the coach from Lindholme dropped us at Elsham and then took them to join their squadron at Waltham. I was overjoyed to see Andy Kelly and we had a long talk over tea and cakes. His tour, it seemed, had been similar to mine but he had an additional 'line' to relate. One night, they were running up on the target when a Lanc. flying just above them released its bomb-load. One of the large incendiaries crashed through the Perspex canopy on to Andy's lap. With great presence of mind and considerable alacrity, he banged open his side window and flung out the unwelcome present.

46

*   *   *

In spite of the persistent rumours which had been circulating for several days, the news that we were to leave Elsham came as a great shock, and a disappointment. We had completed twenty-two operations during our tour of thirty trips and hoped to finish off in a blaze of glory as the veterans of the squadron, loved by many and respected by all. But it was not to be. Certain crews of 103 Squadron, together with crews from two other squadrons, were to fly their aircraft to Kirmington and there form a new Lancaster squadron. The Wellingtons and crews of 166 Squadron, Kirmington, had moved out and all was ready for the new tenants to take over.

We were not alone in our disappointment; 'Yank-in-the-RAF' Drew had done more trips than we had, and he was going, so was Chesterton, with only one more operation needed to complete his tour. It was really tough on 'Ches', especially as several crews had been screened at twenty trips or even less. It did seem a waste of time and effort to send such experienced crews to form a new squadron. There would be all the bind of moving over and settling down, and then, in a matter of a few weeks – or days, in Ches's case – the whole business would have to be repeated when we finished our tours. We consoled ourselves with the surmise that we were being sent to the new outfit to act as a stiffener in the mixture of less-experienced crews who would form the major part of the squadron.

The one outstanding feature of the whole affair was that we were taking 'William'. Dear old 'William'! How valiantly he had played his part since that day when I first saw him standing in dispersal, with the riggers busily painting the squadron and aircraft letters on his fuselage. What a magnificent aeroplane he had been and what a model of refinement and reliability. Naturally, there had been times when all was not well with the old boy and I had, on occasion, referred to him in terms other than complimentary; but then, absolute perfection would be a monotonous thing and even a Lancaster had its faults and peculiarities.

The little white parachute and sea-mine, painted on the nose, which had marked his (and 'Joe's') first successful trip, was followed by an imposing string of miniature bombs, punctuated here and there by larger bombs and ice-cream cones. Each one represented a bombing mission and each had its own little story of thrills and high endeavour, of supreme satisfaction and bitter disappointment.

That first ice-cream cone (derisively representing an Italian trip, the Fascists not being considered worthy of the dignity of a bomb!)

marked a very interesting and extremely dicey raid on Turin. We had looked forward to seeing the snow-clad Alps in the full glory of a moonlit night but had been forced, instead, to fly through violent electrical storms which brought severe icing of airframe and engines, but not one glimpse of the famous peaks. Indeed, there was a period when I feared that our first view of a mountain would be when the jagged rocks of some peak came poking up through the floorboards! Not a few crews were forced to jettison the odd bomb in order to pull back the extra bit of altitude. The attack was very successful and defences – as expected – were soon saturated, although a number of aircraft had trouble and were flown south to airfields in North Africa. The return route was the main snag. We came across Southern France in the half-light of dawn and struck out between La Rochelle and St Nazaire on a long leg into the Atlantic, then turned north-east for Lizard Point. The resultant track miles were prodigious, considering the type of trip and the foul weather we had encountered, and most of the aircraft landed at West Country airfields, having been briefed to do so, if the fuel state was doubtful. To my smug pride, I was able to conserve enough fuel to bring 'William' safely back to base; but this performance was soundly beaten by Chesterton's engineer who brought 'S-Sugar' home with an outboard tank still full of fuel which could not be used because of electric-pump failure. The first aircraft home was Van Rolleghen's 'Z-Zebra', the courageous Belgian having decided to return by the direct route. Only 'Van' could have seen any future in crossing Northern France alone and in daylight. Ken Breckon had engine trouble near the Alps and had to jettison some bombs to gain altitude but was eventually forced to abandon the mission. Although airborne for about seven hours, his effort did not count as an operation. Thirteen crews were missing from the attack and it was rumoured that several others had to ditch, due to lack of petrol.

Our next Italian trip was much more enjoyable. The operation was split into two parts: a straightforward raid on the city of Milan, by Main Force, and a special low-level attack on the Breda-Pirella works, by picked crews. There was no nonsense about the route, straight out and straight home. The weather was glorious throughout the trip, with a full moon riding high in the sky and perfect night visibility, and the Alps were unbelievably beautiful. We crossed at 18,000 feet, then descended to our bombing height of 4,000 feet and, after orbiting the target two or three times, picked out a part of the factory which had not been attacked and planted our bombs smack in the middle of it. We then stooged across Milan, still at the same height, to see how the other lads were faring, and had the usual thrill of watching a city rocked by bombs dropped from 18,000 feet. Defences, by German standards, were very weak, although the light flak in the factory area was fairly good. I spotted a Macchi fighter about a hundred yards to starboard but he seemed to be making for base as quickly as possible – must have learned that the Lancs. were using live ammo! South of the city, we altered course for home and I crowded-on the power in order to regain altitude for re-crossing the Alps. As we climbed, we could see a Lanc. thousands of feet below, swinging in and out of the valleys. He was obviously in trouble and had decided to do things the hard way.

The larger bombs painted on the aircraft, represented trips to the 'Big City'. Our first mission to Berlin had been, as already described, a ten/tenths cloud effort but, three nights later, an all-Lanc. attack had the supreme satisfaction of blitzing the city in perfect weather conditions. That night, the Met. people scored a resounding success. They had forecast ten/tenths cloud on the outward route and clear over the target at zero hour. We confirmed the first part of the forecast as we flew deeper into Germany but began to doubt the second part as we approached the target – the cloud seemed to cover the entire continent. Then, when we had almost resigned ourselves to another 'blind' attack, the cloud finished abruptly, like the unsuspected edge of a precipice, and there was Berlin – unmasked, at our feet, and at our mercy. The defences were terrific but the target was well and truly pranged. The route home caught Jerry napping and, by the time he realised what the score was, we were beyond the reach of his fighters. After bombing, we swept north in the direction of Sweden and then turned west for Denmark and the North Sea. The brightly-lit cities on the Swedish coast gave us quite a thrill, after the blacked-out towns to which we had become accustomed. Some of the lads must have strayed off track to have a closer look, because the Swedes took rather a dim view and demonstrated their neutral anger by throwing up a fair amount of light flak. From every point of view, the trip was a great success and I had more than a little satisfaction in again entering 'BERLIN' in my log-book.

Three of the bombs were painted on in four days – a busy spell. The first two marked the opening stages of the Battle of Hamburg, that series of devastating night and day attacks by the RAF and the United States Eighth Air Force, which wiped out the second-largest city in Germany. The first Hamburg trip was notable for the use of a new counter-measure, known as 'Window', which played havoc with the enemy's system of radiolocation. I cursed the new-fangled strips of metallised paper that first night, because I had the job of dropping them down the flare-chute. Knee deep in packages, fumbling in pitch darkness – having lost my torch – and praying for an electrically-heated suit in place of my battledress, I felt thoroughly miserable. Apart from the intense cold, I hated being down the fuselage and missing all the excitement. However, I did get a good view of that all-devouring sea of flame – the like of which I had never seen before – by taking off one of the bomb-slip covers and peering down through the open bomb-bay during the bombing run. Luckily for my peace of mind, the dropping of 'Window' was afterwards delegated to the bomb aimer, who could perform the task in relative comfort by using a sliding-panel in the Perspex nose, replaced at a later date by a pukka chute on the starboard side of the bombing compartment.

The third trip in the four days was a pin-point attack on a ball-bearing factory at Remscheid, by a small force of Lancasters. There was a double-briefing for the trip, as the major part of the squadron was to visit the Ruhr at approximately the same time as our zero hour, thereby hoping to divide the fighters between the two targets and give us a sporting chance of survival. We liked the arrangement and bliss-fully took off, happy in the knowledge that the rest of the boys were 'right behind us'. The trip was very exciting and we got caught up in some pretty deadly heavy flak; 'William', however, seemed quite unruffled by the stuff and I presumed that the damage, if any, was of a minor character. Thankful to get away from the target in one piece, it was in a very good frame of mind that we re-crossed the enemy coast, *en route* for our bacon and eggs. After checking the fuel state, I turned to look through the window and was somewhat shocked to see a huge sheet of flame engulf the starboard-outer engine. Instinctively, I operated the propeller-feathering switch, engine master-cock, throttle and pitch levers, and the fire-extinguisher button; during which time I warned Reg and the rest of the crew of the position – not that they needed any warning, the blaze must have been visible for miles. Fortunately, the fire died out as quickly as it had started. We would have been in real trouble if it had persisted for, being over the sea, there was not much point in baling out and, as we were still at 18,000 feet, a ditching was impossible in the time available. But all was well and we made base quite comfortably on three engines. A jagged hole in the engine-cowling bore testimony to the accuracy of the Jerry flak, which had damaged the coolant system

– providing an unwelcome thrill for Bunten and crew, and a new engine for 'William'. At debriefing, we learned that the supporting effort had been scrubbed shortly after we had taken off. The remarks of the Remscheid crews were worth hearing!

One of the bombs represented a trip on which we did not actually attack the target – for very good reasons! The night of 2 August 1943 was to be the concluding chapter in the story of the Battle of Hamburg. Photographic reconnaissance had shown widespread devastation in the built-up area and in the shipbuilding yards, but so dense was the smoke from the burning city that it was impossible to obtain a true picture of the full effects of previous raids and it was therefore decided to lay on a final attack. At briefing, the Met. Officer warned us of a 'front' lying across the North Sea, which might give trouble on the outward route but was not expected to affect the target area until long after our zero hour. Soon after crossing the home coast, we ran into the 'front' and decided to climb over it. The decision was easy to make but not quite so easy to accomplish. We climbed and climbed but could not shake off the enveloping cloud, the 'front' had no ceiling. There was no alternative but to press on and wait for the forecast break. Visibility was practically nil and, after a while, I got the impression that we were flying through a dark tunnel, in which several hundred other aircraft were also flying – aircraft which we would not see until it was too late to avoid a collision. As we stooged along, little blue lights of static electricity began to dance across the framework of our cockpit windows; Reg looked at me and gave me a thumbs-down sign. Suddenly, a terrific flash split the darkness, followed by several more at short intervals. The 'front' was beginning to show its teeth! The static increased in severity and when I looked out of the windows, I saw a fantastic sight. Each propeller track formed a huge foot-thick circle of vivid blue light; guns, aerials, windows and air-intake grills flickered with gremlinesque lights; and from each wingtip a vicious, yards-long, blue electric flame licked back into the slipstream. We roared steadily on, waiting for the moment when we broke cloud into more normal conditions. But the electrical storm was only just getting into its stride! Almost imperceptibly, a thin film of white began to creep along the edges of the windows and a glance outside confirmed my fears, the air-intake grills and the leading-edge of the mainplane were also turning white – we were starting to pick up ice. There was only one thing to be done about icing and that was to get out of it as quickly as possible. Unfortunately, we couldn't climb out of it and we didn't relish the idea of going down into worse conditions – so we pressed on regardless. Our carburettor-intake control was already in 'Hot Air' but, in spite of this precaution, the needles of the engine-revolution indicators began to flicker and the boost-pressure gauges registered an alarming amount of boost-surge. In sympathy with the surge, the four Merlins throbbed in and out of sychronisation and poor 'William' began to lurch about the sky. We tried everything, but the port engines got worse every minute and the airframe was shaking like a leaf in the wind. The situation was rapidly getting out of hand.

A few miles short of the target, 'William' gave a convulsive shudder, turned over on to his port side and then fell clean out of the sky. For a few moments, the cockpit personnel were in a state of slight confusion, but when everyone had regained their composure and sorted out the tangled intercom-leads and oxygen-tubes, we realised that all was not lost. Reg was having a tough time fighting the controls, so I slammed down the bomb-door lever and Corky jettisoned the bomb-load as soon as the doors opened. I then 'feathered' both port engines and increased power on the starboards, and turned to help Reg at the control column. Hamburg was forgotten in the struggle and it was only after losing several thousand feet that we regained control of the aircraft and were able to re-shuffle our thoughts. We hated the idea of wasting the bombs – especially as we were so close to the target – but consoled ourselves with the thought that they were dropped on German territory and might possibly have done some damage. Bill gave us a course for home and we staggered along on the starboard engines, gradually losing height and still in that filthy cloud. We were about half-way across the North Sea when we eventually ran out of the 'front' and shortly afterwards I was able to restart one of the port engines and we finally made base in good order. Eddie was the first man out of the aircraft, he ran to the grass at the side of the dispersal and reverently kissed the ground.

There were some very angry crews at interrogation. Practically every aircraft had been in dire distress with engines cutting right out and hardly anybody claimed to have bombed the target. To the question, 'What did you bomb?' the general answer was, 'North-West Germany!' It was later reported that thirty aircraft had been lost on the operation. Someone had 'boobed' and, as usual, the Bomber Boys 'carried the can'.

*   *   *

I had been at Elsham for just over four months and had thoroughly enjoyed myself. Life on an operational squadron had far exceeded my expectations, there was something about it which got into my blood. Until the end of my days, the words, 'Elsham Wolds' and '103 Squadron' would bring back a flood of memories. In the main they would be happy memories but there would also be sad memories of gallant crews and true friends who had failed to make the return trip. I could never forget those grand lads skippered by Bob Cant, Ken Breckon, Johnny Stoneman, and all the others. Of the crews which had left Lindholme in such jubilation during the early part of May, bound for squadrons at Elsham, Binbrook, Ludford Magna and Waltham, so very few remained.

The Avro designers would have been horrified to see the amount of stuff we pushed into 'William's' fuselage and bomb-bay when we took off from Elsham for the last time. There were at least twenty kit-bags, six bicycles, piles of flying clothing, suitcases, radios, bomb-winches, wheel chocks, engine-covers, cans of dope, tool kits, an assortment of heavy equipment which the ground crew insisted on taking along, and – crowded into the few vacant spaces – eleven men. Rather sadly, we taxied from dispersal point for the last time. Past Van Rolleghen's 'Z-Zebra' with its crossed British and Belgian flags, and past the point where Bob Cant's 'U-Uncle', with its pawn-shop sign of the three brass balls, used to stand. Slowly round the perimeter track we moved, in company with Chesterton, in 'S-Sugar', and Drew, in 'T-Tommy'. Ches's kite was better known as 'The Cank Box' and was famous for the amazing collection of lucky charms in the cockpit; for the poster pasted on the wall opposite the door, 'Is your journey really necessary?'; and for the wooden notice-board over the Elsan, 'Passengers are requested not to use this seat whilst the train is standing in the station.' Drew's kite, known as 'Dante's Daughter', took its name from the painting on the side of the nose, showing a life-size nude, with a bomb in each hand, rising from the flames of an inferno.

There was a crowd of well-wishers at the end of the runway and, as Reg swung 'William' into position, I acknowledged their cheers by giving the old thumbs-up sign and then turned to concentrate on the take-off – our last from Elsham.

The spirit of the Wellington squadron hovered over Kirmington for several days and it seemed to me that the station was somewhat over-awed by the arrival of the Lancasters. We were fortunate in getting a good ground crew to tend 'William' but several of the other crews had to remind their boys that it was intended to build '166' into a 'gen' squadron, renowned for successful sorties and reliable aircraft. Of course, we realised that there would be some difficulty in settling down, especially as Kirmington was not fully equipped for servicing and that all replacements and major repairs would have to be handled by Elsham.

We were surprised to meet George Ferrell at Kirmington. He was the mid-upper in the old Ken Breckon crew but had recently negotiated a transfer to the United States Army Air Corps and was wearing slinky American uniform when we met him. His posting had just come through and we had a pleasant farewell party in the Mess on the strength of his greatly increased pay-packet.

Three days after our arrival, we were briefed to attack Hanover, and 'William' was to be the first Lancaster to take off from Kirmington on an operational mission. Unfortunately, our start was delayed by a spot of trouble with the starboard-inner engine and Chesterton, in 'Sugar', had the honour of leading the new squadron into the air. The attack was very successful and we raced home to be on the premises when Ches and his boys came in for the last debriefing of their tour. There would certainly be high jinks in the Mess afterwards and Ches could be relied upon to make the crew's screening celebration an event to be remembered.

After our interrogation, we hung around until it became evident that the famous 'Cank Box' would not be home that night. On his last trip, Ches had failed to return to base. Of course, there was the hope that he had landed away or had ditched in the North Sea but we could not shake off the feeling that the absence was permanent. Never again, we feared, would the Ante Room ring to the strains of the Chesterton crew's version of *Deutschland über Alles*:

> 'We take off as daylight's fading,
> For to Germany we must go,
> Flying o'er at twenty thousand,
> Fighters above and flak below;
> Cologne–Wuppertal–Bochum–Dusseldorf,
> They are just an awful mess!
> Berlin–Hanover–Mannheim–Hamburg,
> "All aboard!" for the "Deutschland Express"!'

On our next trip, we returned from Mannheim on three engines and – coupling this incident with our delayed start on the previous trip, and one or two minor snags on air tests – we began to wonder if we were running into a spell of bad luck. It was, therefore, with some trepidation that we gained height over base on our second trip to Hanover, especially as we were due to go on leave on our return. I felt very uneasy. There was definitely something wrong with our 'William'. I could feel it in my bones. And yet, there was no indication that the engines were likely to give trouble. Soon after setting course, the gremlins got to work on 'William'; the port-outer began to surge and the fuel pressure warning light flickered on for a few seconds and then went out. At 14,000 feet over the North Sea, the surge increased and the engine-revolution indicator, after fluctuating violently for several minutes, returned to the zero position. The loss of a rev-counter was a minor detail and we just carried on, hoping that the engine would clear itself. I tried all the dodges, but could not effect any improvement. Suddenly, the needle of the boost-pressure gauge went berserk and oscillated between the readings of '–4'and '+10'; fourteen pounds of boost surge! It was unbelievable! In sympathy with the surge, the exhaust flames were alternately licking back past the mid-upper turret and dying away into the exhaust-stubs. 'William' was being heavily punished and there was no future in pressing on. On the decision to abandon the mission, I feathered the engine, Reg opened the bomb-doors, Corky jettisoned the bombs into the sea, and we turned for home.

An abortive sortie was never popular and we felt rather like truant schoolboys as we reported to the CO and the Squadron Engineering Officer. The story of our trouble sounded like a whimsy from Grimm's Fairy Tales and the Engineer Officer winced as I spoke of 'Fourteen pounds boost-surge' – the fact that we were going on leave in a few hours did nothing to help matters. (See Appendix 2)

After breakfast, I hurried down to dispersal. 'Taffy', one of our engine fitters, was just taking off the cowlings as I arrived and I heard him give a whistle of amazement. Climbing on to the engine stand, I gazed in awe at the horrible mess of burned and twisted metal that had once been a beautiful Merlin engine. There was a series of jagged holes where the exhaust stubs had torn away from the cylinder head on the port side; the supercharger casing had a great hole burned in its side; bent control rods and cables lay on a filthy, sticky mess of charred fuel and oil pipelines; and the rear of the engine looked as though it had been subjected to intense heat treatment and had then been hammered by a madman.

It was enough! We were vindicated! I rushed to find the Engineer

Officer, and at the subsequent inquest on the deceased engine we agreed that the exhaust stubs had worked loose on their studs (probably due to the burning of a faulty gasket) and had finally pulled away from the head, allowing the exhaust flames to pour into the inside of the cowling; the terrific heat had burned through the fuel-pressure light switch and the rev-counter drive, and had then attacked the blower casing and the boost-regulator unit. The explanation fitted the symptoms perfectly but nobody could understand why the whole thing hadn't just gone up in flames.

With clear consciences and reputation unsullied, we prepared for leave.

Four more operations: Stuttgart; Hanover; Hanover; and Leipzig had been entered into our log-books since the abortive Hanover mission, and we began to look forward to the completion of our tour.

Our twenty-ninth trip was to Kassel, an important town at the 'back' of the Ruhr. Never before had I been so thrilled by an attack. It had everything. The target area, especially, was seething with excitement. We saw fighter flares, searchlights, 'scarecrows', light and heavy flak, red TIs and green TIs, dummy firesights, dense columns of smoke, raging fires, burning aircraft falling out of the sky, and a swarm of enemy night fighters darting in and out of the bomber stream. 'William' was in superb form and he swept round the route with the nonchalant air of one who is completely master of the situation. On the leg out of the target, I witnessed an amazing occurrence. A running battle had been taking place, way over to starboard, and the all-too-familiar glowing ball told of another Lancaster which would not return to base. I waited to see the usual falling inferno and the subsequent breaking up of the aircraft but instead I saw the orange glow increase in size and maintain its altitude. The glow came nearer and nearer, and I realised that it was heading in our direction. As it approached, I was able to make out the shape of the aircraft and could see that it *was* a Lanc. slowly banking over to port. Reg eased 'William' out of range as the doomed Lancaster tore past our starboard wing-tip, with only a few yards to spare. It was a fantastic sight: the port side was ablaze from stem to stern and, with terrific flames fanning out into the slipstream, it looked like a hideous torch. I tried to make out the squadron letters but this proved impossible, as the starboard side was silhouetted against the glare. I watched it continue its circle of death until the inevitable happened and the agonised Lancaster exploded and dropped slowly to earth in a thousand burning pieces.

Forty-four aircraft were reported missing from the operation. 'Wally' Hammond and crew were amongst those who did not return. We were very sorry about this because they had been with us at Elsham and were great friends of ours. On the previous day, Reg and I had gone over to Elsham and, on meeting Hammond, who had gone to collect a kite, were offered a lift back to Kirmington. I rode in the rear turret for a change but was glad when we touched-down – I didn't care for the loneliness, and kept swinging the turret to satisfy myself that it was still attached to the rest of the aircraft! Good old 'Wally'! I hoped that everything had gone well with them but I could not shake off the memory of that blazing Lanc. and, in a way, felt glad that I had been unable to make out the squadron letters. The odds were against it being Hammond's kite but I couldn't help wondering. Still, even if it had been his, the lads had bags of time to bale out and the behaviour of the aircraft did suggest to me that the occupants had put 'George' in control before making their escape.

Ten days had elapsed since the Kassel raid and still we hadn't logged that last, elusive trip. Two or three attacks had been scrubbed and we began to feel frustrated but on the morning of 2 November 1943, however, we felt that the great day had arrived: the very atmosphere reeked of action and the 'jungle telegraph' had informed us that an op was a cast-iron certainty. We prepared our equipment with extra care and then nipped over to the crew-room to find out the score from Reg. The other skippers were already rounding up their crews but Reg was still closeted with the Flight Commander. Eventually, he came striding down the corridor and the look on his face was worth the waiting – obviously, we were 'on' and we began to press for details. For a while, Reg just stood there, smiling. Then, in a quiet voice, he said, 'We are *not* operating . . .'.

In the pause that followed, Eddie expressed himself in a few choice Canadian swear-words and the rest of us groaned as one. Of all the confounded luck! Why, for Pete's sake, had we been 'stood down' on this day of days?

Still smiling, and enjoying the effect of his words on the boys, Reg walked towards the crew-room door and then, as he stood in the open doorway, he turned and completed his sentence, '. . . because the CO has just informed me that we have been screened'!

As the 'green' flashed from the checkered caravan, 'William' rolled slowly forward, gathering speed as the throttles were progressively opened. Soon, he was tearing down the runway and then, as the pilot eased him off the deck, he tucked his legs up and slipped away into the evening dusk.

With something more than a hint of tears in my eyes, I tucked 'Joe', who had also been watching the take-off, into my battledress and turned to Reg and the other boys. They were staring in the direction of the fast-disappearing aircraft and I felt that they, also, were profoundly moved. The gallant 'William', our well-beloved 'William', would never again be coupled with the name 'BUNTEN' on the Squadron Battle Order. Our totally-unexpected screening had been wonderful news and we were very excited, but we had not reckoned on the sorrow of parting from the aircraft which had been the sure foundation on which we had built our tour. Bunten and crew would soon be leaving for pastures new, to find welcome relief from the strain of operational flying, but 'William' would have to press on regardless.

As we walked along to our billets, we watched the grim, black shapes overhead and listened to the throbbing beat of their engines: they were heading in a south-easterly direction, flying very high and still climbing. My thoughts went back to that spring evening at Binbrook, when I had first seen the 'heavies' going out on a mission and had wondered what the future might hold. Now our tour was ended and Fate had indeed been kind.

The public telephone was 'out of bounds' on the day of an operation and, in consequence, I waited until the first returning aircraft roared over the 'drome before I called up Dot to give her the news of our screening. Naturally, she was delighted and I asked her to arrange for immediate leave. Conversation was rather difficult because of the noise of the Lancasters circling overhead but we didn't mind in the least, the roaring of the Merlins lent a touch of romance to the occasion. Everything was going to be fine; Dot would get fourteen days 'marriage leave' and I expected at least fourteen days 'screening leave'. We planned to marry as soon as possible after returning home, so that we could devote the remainder of our leave to the honeymoon. I returned to the billet feeling that all was well with the world, at any rate, with my world.

Next morning, I sent a telegram to the folks at home. At first, I was undecided whether this was wise or not, because a telegram from an operational station so often commenced with the words, 'We regret to inform you . . .' Still, I felt sure that they would already have learned, through the mysterious thing we call telepathy, that their worries were over for the present.

During the morning, the boys and I had an interview with the Squadron CO. He congratulated us on our screening and spoke in glowing terms of our highly-successful tour. Our posting-notices had come through and he gave us our individual instructions. Bill, Corky and I were going to Hixon; Eddie to Ossington; Doug to Wymeswold; and Reg Boys to Whitchurch; the skipper was staying with the squadron, pending further instructions. We were all to proceed on leave immediately.

We smiled at each other. The prospect of a six months' screening period was very pleasant and we would have an excellent opportunity of resting mind and body before undertaking a second tour of ops. Not that life would be just a glorious holiday but that we would be able to aviate with comparative ease, without being chivvied around by flak or night fighters. And, of course, there was the fourteen days' leave – or would it be longer? Reg queried the point.

The CO picked up the 'signal' from his desk and, without looking up, said, 'You have been given forty-eight hours'. He could not fail to see that we were furious, as he stood up to shake hands, and proffered to contact Group and ask them to extend our leave, but he was not optimistic.

We were gloomily sipping our coffee in the Ante Room when Reg brought the news that the CO had wangled seven days for us. The effect was terrific, we began to feel that life was worth living after all.

I was going to miss the free-and-easy atmosphere of an ops squadron and, as I began to pack away my flying clothing, I realised that I was also going to miss the thrills of the actual missions. There had been so much excitement and interest that my mind was filled with a jumble of memories which had no connection with any particular trip but formed a hazy background of incidents to the more definite highlights of our tour.

As article followed article into the kit-bag, I thought back to the days at Aldergrove and St Athan. My chances of survival had then seemed very remote and the realisation of my ambitions, a fanciful dream. But since those days, I had completed a tour of twenty-nine operations and two abortive sorties, without suffering so much as a scratch. And this, in times when scarcely one man in three could hope to survive a tour; often a tour of only twenty ops or even less. I had been very lucky.

I picked up our little mascot, 'Joe,' and tenderly packed him away.

He had borne himself bravely in many a tight corner and I resolved, there and then, that for the rest of my life, wherever I went, 'Joe' would always go with me.

At Barnetby railway station, the boys and I stood in a group and waited for the train which would take us our different ways. Seven men who were more like brothers than friends. I looked at each of the boys in turn, as though to impress his features on my heart. How happy we had been and how successful our association. Each man indispensable in his own capacity, carrying out his duties to the very best of his abilities, and always ready to put the welfare of the crew before all else. To Reg, Eddie, Reg Boys and Doug, it was 'Goodbye'; Corky, Bill and I would meet again at Hixon. With a heavy heart, I realised that the days of 'Bunten and crew, in "W-for-William"', were over.

Chapter Four

Screened

Returning to duty, after a spot of leave, was never a pleasant business and as I sat in the crowded compartment of the Euston train, I reflected on my unhappy lot. For quite a time I was subjected to the same feelings of baffled rage and resentment which must have afflicted the victims of the press-gangs of old. The mood could not last, however, and under the soothing influence of the 'fragrant weed' my thoughts turned to pleasant memories of the previous week.

Dot and I, assisted by the folks, had spent the first day of leave, making final arrangements for our wedding. There was so much to do and so little time to do it in, that we felt certain that things would be in a hopeless mix-up on the day. As usually happens when one fears the worst, everything went according to plan and immediately after the reception, Dot and I left for our honeymoon.

Four days may not seem long for a honeymoon but we thoroughly enjoyed ourselves. Whilst strolling down the promenade at Blackpool, we met Cyril Greenhough, a home-town friend, who was a Corporal Instructor at the Squire's Gate training unit. Cyril and I had last met at Gloucester on the Fitter's Course and we had to chat about our experiences during the intervening years. Strangely enough, he had recently been stationed at Hixon and was able to give me quite a lot of useful gen on the place.

One evening, we were in a cinema when the newsreel showed scenes after an Investiture at Buckingham Palace. Several newly-decorated heroes posed in front of the camera and then I was delighted to see my good friend, George Ferrell, appear on the screen. He was proudly displaying the Distinguished Flying Medal which had been awarded for his skill and daring on that dicey first trip with Ken Breckon and crew. How well I remembered the head-lines in the morning papers on the day following the Dortmund attack, 'FOUR-ENGINED BOMBER GETS HOME ON ONE!' I

61

The author with his bride, Doris 'Dot' Ashton

fell to wondering what had happened to Ken and his boys, and thought how little we ever learned about the fate of missing crews.

I was rudely awakened from my day-dreams by the screech of brakes and the deep tones of a station announcer calling, 'Stafford! Stafford! This is Stafford!' I hastily collected my kit and descended to the platform, feeling much more contented than when I had joined the train. After all, there was a war on.

On arrival at Hixon, I soon found myself amongst friends. Bill and Corky were there and I also met two engineer pals from Elsham who 'gave me the griff' on the type of work I would be expected to do. As far as I could gather, my duties would mainly be confined to technical instruction and air/sea rescue drills. There seemed little chance of getting airborne. I did not feel too confident of making good as an instructor, especially as the crews were being trained on Wellington aircraft, about which I knew practically nothing. Still, I was prepared to have a go.

My first week passed very quickly and I learned quite a lot about the Wellington, or 'Wimpy' as it was affectionately known to the RAF, a nickname derived from the character in the 'Popeye' cartoons, J. Wellington Wimpy. I studied the aircraft and its equipment; the various drills in connection with the engines; the oxygen equipment; air/sea rescue drills and equipment, parachute drills; fire drills; and the thousand-and-one things that go to make up the complex business of successful aviation. The really tough job, however, was to forget my Lancaster gen temporarily and overcome my four-engine complex in order to concentrate on the new stuff, but I began to feel that I was making progress. The 'Wimpy' and I were going to be great friends.

During the week, news had come through that Reg Bunten had been awarded the DFC and Bill Bailey, the DFM; Reg had also been commissioned. I was delighted at the great honour bestowed on our skipper and navigator, and felt that these awards were well deserved, for the success of our tour had been largely due to the splendid work of both boys. And, of course, the awards reflected credit on the rest of the crew.

I had been at Hixon almost a fortnight when the officer in charge of the section sent for me and asked me if I would like to go over to the satellite 'drome at Seighford and reorganise the Airmanship Section at that station. I demurred at first but secretly felt rather pleased at the confidence shown in such a new boy – or was I being palmed off with a very troublesome baby? I was assured that everything was on the level. Hixon was not satisfied with the way things were going at Seighford and decided that the place needed new blood and fresh thinking. With all the confidence in the world, I accepted the chance – and the challenge.

I liked Seighford from the very moment I stepped out of the crewcoach which had brought me over from Hixon. And I soon found that I had gained a good friend in Geoff Battersby, my partner in the section. He had done a tour on Stirlings and was familiar with 'Hercules' engines; the type used also on Wellingtons.

In a few weeks, we had transformed the once-uninteresting and uninspiring Nissen hut into a bright, well-equipped and inviting Airmanship Section. We had organised a system of progressive lectures for all crew categories; established good relations with the various aircrew and ground staff sections; and gained respect for the subjects we taught. Above all, we had succeeded in winning the interest of the pupils; especially the pilots, who began to treat the section as their own particular spot. The people at Hixon paid one or two strategic visits and expressed themselves as more than satisfied with the progress made. It was, therefore, with a modicum of pride that I took my first leave from No. 30 Operational Training Unit and journeyed homewards for the New Year.

When I heard the news that we were to have an officer in charge of the section, I was somewhat peeved. Trust the commissioned types to walk in and take all the credit when the hard work had been done! But when I met the officer in question, I realised at once that he was definitely going to be a welcome addition. Flight Lieutenant 'Chalky' White was a screened pilot who had done a tour of ops on 'Wimps' in the Middle East. He was enthusiastic about his job as an instructor, both in the air and on the deck, and assured us that he had every intention of pulling his weight in the section. We soon became firm friends and made great plans to further widen the scope of our training activities.

Usually, there were two 'courses', comprising thirty crews in all, at Seighford. The senior course in, say, 'B' Flight, would be doing night-flying and the junior course, in 'D' Flight, day-flying. On completing their training, the seniors were posted to HCU for conversion to four-engined stuff; the 'D' Flight crews would become senior course and commence night-flying, whilst a new course would join 'B' Flight for day-flying. Thus we had an influx of fifteen crews, ninety men, every few weeks. At the Airmanship Section, we tried to maintain contact with the crews throughout their stay by means of our lectures and drills during non-flying periods. Our ambition was to ensure that every crew member could cope not only with his own particular job in the aircraft but could, in an emergency, deputise for any comrade who might be injured or otherwise incapacitated. In the hangar we had a complete Wellington fuselage and in this we taught individual crews how to ditch and bale out. We insisted on the drills being carried out in full flying clothing and those boys certainly perspired. At Stafford Public Baths, we showed them how to handle dinghies and Mae Wests in the water, and how to cope with the difficulties they would undoubtedly meet in an actual ditching. In the decompression chamber, we brought home to them the vital importance of correct oxygen procedure and proved to each man that, at operational altitude, lack of oxygen could be just as deadly as a burst of flak or cannon-shell.

Personally, I had never worked so hard in my life but it was well worth while. Often I would lecture for seven hours a day, take a late night-flying briefing and then talk 'shop' with the pupils in the Ante Room till midnight. For me, the 'hangar doors' were never closed. Normally, bods under training were only too glad to call it a day at tea-time but, over and over again, my boys would corner me in the Mess and drag me into a full-blooded discussion on some question that was puzzling them. I asked no greater compliment. They were taking us, and their jobs, seriously and that was the really important thing.

The Sergeants' Mess was comparatively primitive, as Messes go, but the lack of amenities was amply compensated for by the general atmosphere of homeliness and good fellowship. There were some grand types among the instructors and ground staff NCOs and I made many good friends. The majority of the aircrew chaps had operated in Lancs from this country but there were also several who had done their tours in 'Wimps' from the Middle East. Not that we Lanc. types would ever admit that a Middle East tour could really be classed as operational flying – our mocking advice to them was to 'Get some Ruhr-bashing hours in'! It was very, very pleasant on a winter's night to sit yarning and shooting lines round a roaring fire; many thrilling experiences were recounted and interesting trips recalled to mind.

One evening, I was amazed to see a once-familiar figure come walking into the Ante Room. It was Syd Horton, wireless operator in the Bob Cant crew which failed to return from the raid on Mannheim. I had heard rumours from time to time that certain members of the crew were safe but this was news in the flesh! Syd was not only safe, and looking disgustingly fit, but had been posted to Seighford as a Signals Instructor. And what a story he had to tell.

'U-Uncle' had made her attack on the target and was settling down for the run home from Mannheim, when one of the engines started misfiring badly and the aircraft became unmanageable. Bob ordered the crew to abandon aircraft. (Syd smiled at my puzzled frown and then whimsically explained that they had arrived at the target on three engines, had lost another over the target and the misfiring left them with only one good engine!) On the order to bale out, Syd made his way down the fuselage and departed with no little haste from the rear exit. He remembered to pull the string and the parachute opened perfectly; apart from a sensation of going up instead of down, the descent to earth was uneventful. After spilling and retrieving his 'chute, Syd sat down on enemy soil and waited for something to happen. Soon, he heard the low whistling of a still lower song, 'Salome', and the whistler could only be one of his crew mates. Syd crept on all-fours in the direction of the sound and saw the stocky figure of the rear gunner, unmistakable even in the gloom. Bob Parkinson had also made a good landing and after a futile search for the rest of the crew, both boys took counsel on their plans for the immediate future. They decided to stick together and make for home by the quickest route, so parachutes and harnesses were hidden in a ditch and stock was taken of their equipment. Like all good ops types, they each carried escape-kits and purses, and had a good reserve of emergency rations. By calculating the flying time, speed and direction from the target, they were able to form a rough estimate of their position on the map and figured that they were in Luxembourg. After checking direction by the aid of an escape-compass and the stars, they turned west and set course for home.

I sat enthralled as Syd unfolded the story of their journey across Occupied Europe – not the complete story, of course, because the security people insisted on certain details being kept secret.

There was, it seemed, reliable news of the remaining crew members; with the exception of the bomb aimer, Dennis Teare, of whom nothing was known. Bob Cant, along with Dicky Dickson, the flight engineer, and Bill Milburn, the mid-upper gunner, had successfully evaded and gained sanctuary in Switzerland. A recent letter from them had conveyed the impression that a pleasant time was being had by all. The navigator, Tommy Thomas, had unfortunately been captured after a spell of freedom and was in a POW camp in Germany. I thought this was a terrific performance: five successful evaders out of a crew of seven, and perhaps another to come!

Not only was I glad to hear this wonderful news but I also felt cheered by its implications. If Bob and his boys were safe, why not a goodly number of the other missing crews? And what of the possibility of Jack Osborne being alive? The Red Cross organisation had recently informed Jack's mother that although the bomb aimer was reported POW, the remainder of the crew had been killed and were buried in Holland. The bomb aimer had written from the camp to say that he baled out and did not know what had happened to the others. In spite of this information, I felt there was still an outside chance that Jack had escaped and was in hiding with the underground movement.

It was in the middle of January that I heard I was going to Bristol for a short course on 'Hercules' engines. The news was very welcome because, although I had worked on air-cooled radials at Aldergrove, my operational experience had been on liquid-cooled in-line 'Merlins'. Certainly I had picked up a lot of gen at Hixon and Seighford but I felt glad of the chance to learn the finer points of the performance and maintenance of the famous sleeve-valve engine.

The course was taken in a very fine building, originally a school for blind children, which had been wonderfully equipped for training RAF personnel by the Bristol Aeroplane Company. The instructors had all worked in the Bristol engine-shops and were real gen-men on the subject. During the fortnight I was there, I was taught practically everything I could wish to know about the 'Hercules' and considered the course one of the best I had ever taken.

There were several flight engineers on the course and I became very friendly with two of them in particular, Jock McDonald and Bert Radford. Jock had the usual Scottish habit of grousing but, like most Scots, he didn't mean the half of it. He was a 'regular' so of course he groused about the Service; he had done a tour on Stirlings, so he groused about operations and about Stirlings. He loved to disparage himself above all. Vowed he would go 'LMF' if only he had the guts! He claimed that his crew never actually went to a target but did a split turn several miles away and skidded the bombs in! Stirlings were terrible and their kite was the worst of the lot – swore they could never climb high enough to warrant the use of oxygen, and grumbled that not only had they to put up with the light flak – which did not trouble us – but suffered agonies from near-misses by shot-down Lancasters floating past in flames. A born grumbler was Jock, but let anyone else attack the Service, operating, Stirlings or himself and he would immediately leap into the argument and defend them. Having many friends from north of the border, I soon saw through his manner and accepted his grousing at its true worth.

Bert Radford was also a decent type, rather quiet at Bristol but I gathered that he had been having a spot of sickness and was taking things easy. He had operated on Lancs. and had been in one or two 'sticky do's' during his tour. There was one chap there that I seemed to recognise but could not place until we had a chat and found that we had been at Kirkham together in 1940. Fred Jenner was the second man I had contacted since those days; the other was Andy Kelly who had also been with me at Lindholme.

The school had a clubroom in one of the outbuildings and it was there I saw a very interesting relic of the 1914–18 war; an aero engine of the rotary type. Although the design and workmanship was, no doubt, excellent for the period in which it was built, I couldn't help admiring the courage of men who had flown in combat with aircraft powered by such flimsy devices.

My visit to Bristol was soon reflected on the gen-boards which covered the walls of our section and I lost no time in incorporating the latest griff in my lectures. Some of the pilots were keenly interested in the theoretical side of engine performance and I was thankful to be able to supply them with the makers' facts and figures. It seemed to me that the quality of pilots was improving, enginewise, and I ascribed this to the policy of using flight engineers as instructors. I also thought that we were getting better material from Hixon, where the Airmanship people had recently installed a test engine. This was a wizard set-up, complete with pilot's cockpit connected to and controlling the engine, accumulators and a charging set, and flowmeters to demonstrate to pilots how fuel consumption was affected by the correct and incorrect operation of the various engine controls.

One of our senior courses, after a series of 'Bullseye' trips, was looking forward to the final exercise; a leaflet raid on France, known as a 'Nickel'. Geoff and I were kept busy by crews who wanted to check up on their emergency drills and by pilots doing a spot of revision on trouble flying. Instead of flying over home territory, playing hide-and-seek with friendly searchlights for the edification of themselves and the AA and searchlight batteries, they would be making their bow on the European stage, where the only bouquets presented to them would be jagged lumps of hot metal. Instead of dropping tiny practice bombs on well-defined targets, they would be delivering copies of *Le Courrier de l'Air* to the people who were anxiously awaiting the opening of the long-talked-of Second Front. One or two crews made light of this last exercise of their training but I warned them to treat it with the seriousness of a pukka mission. You never could tell, even on a 'Nickel'.

At the briefing, I repeated the warning. The trip seemed straightforward enough but I had a feeling that there was going to be trouble.

And there was! In fact, there was very nearly a shambles. Of the six crews detailed, only one returned to base in good order. The other five had to resort to emergency procedures of various kinds and must have had occasion to remember my words. One crew had engine trouble over the Continent and were faced with a probable ditching in the Channel. They carried out distress procedure correctly and went through the drills we had taught them in the dummy fuselage; fortunately, they had plenty of height when the engine packed up and they were able to make the home coast without undue worry. But their troubles were by no means over. The ground was covered by ten/tenths cloud and they couldn't find a 'drome; then the pilot found that the petrol situation was getting serious and realised that they had to get down pretty soon – or else! They did eventually get down, but not in the Wellington. No 'drome could be found and there was no alternative but to head the aircraft out to sea and bale out. Everyone made a good landing with the exception of the rear gunner, who crocked an ankle when he dropped on a patch of rough ground.

Three aircraft made emergency landings away from base, two had engine trouble which necessitated single-engined landings and the third had to lob down in a hurry because one of his fuel tanks had been damaged by flak, with a consequent loss of fuel. One of the 'single-engine' crews had been attacked by an Fw 190 which was dealt with in masterly fashion by the rear gunner, who promptly smacked it down with a short burst at point-blank range. This effort really shook our Gunnery Section people because they had taken a very dim view of that particular gunner and had almost scrubbed him from the course. The pilot of the Fockewulf doubtless wished that they had done so, for what glory was there in being shot down by a trainee?

The fifth aircraft to experience trouble got caught up in a heap of flak and had its fuselage well and truly plastered. The skipper managed to hold the kite together and staggered back to base, finally bringing it down to a very fine landing. The crew were unharmed (as were all the crews that night) but the 'Wimp' was a complete write-off.

All crews coped extremely well with their various troubles and we Airmanship types came in for some high praise from the CO and lots of thanks from the 'Nickel' boys.

Of particular interest to me were the all-too-frequent crashes which marred the work of operational training and, where possible, I found out the reasons for the crashes and included them as warning examples in my lectures and drills. I had found that pupils learned more from the actual 'boobs' and 'blacks' put up by other crews than from hazy conjectures as to what *might* happen. Especially did I make play with the ditching statistic of Wellington and Lancaster aircraft, drawing comparison between the number of men involved in known ditchings and the number actually rescued. The figures were rather frightening. So long as the continental coast remained the enemy coast, ditching was an ever-present possibility to an operational crew and I never allowed the boys to lose sight of that fact.

I travelled to Northern Ireland for my next leave and enjoyed the trip over, even the once-depressing boat journey from Heysham to Belfast seemed good fun; but then, I never had a wife to greet me in the old Aldergrove days. Dot was stationed at Whitehead, on the northern shore of Belfast Lough, and had arranged for us to stay at a bungalow hard by the Ack-Ack site.

The arrival of a Bomber Boy had evidently been noised abroad, for on the following day I had an invitation from Lieutenant Junor, of 499 HAA Battery, to inspect the site. I thoroughly enjoyed the experience and spent a very pleasant and informative afternoon amongst the guns and predictors, rounding off a nice spot of liaison by taking tea in the Sergeants' Mess. Lieutenant Junor assured me that everything would be done to give my wife as much time off duty as possible during my stay – a very fine gesture. The Army was never slow to seize an opportunity and, after tea, I was contacted by Major Saunders who asked me if I would give a lecture to the troops on the following day – a request I could hardly refuse, in the circumstances. Not that I wanted to refuse, anyhow, for I liked talking about Service life and especially about flying.

I duly arrived for the line-shooting session, only to find that pay parade for the men had been moved forward a day and, in spite of efforts to alter the time of the parade – an amazing compliment – it would not be possible for the men to attend the lecture in a body. Profuse apologies were made and, rather than interfere with another day of my leave, I was asked if I would lecture to the ATS. That was rather more than I had bargained for, but I had become so accustomed to talking for hours on end that I would not have turned a hair if asked to cope with a roomful of Chinese coolies.

There were between forty and fifty girls in my audience and very charming they were. I spotted Jessie Dixon, Betty Thompson and several more of Dot's friends. Obviously I would have to weigh my words with care for there was sure to be some tale-telling in the barrack room afterwards. Dot was on duty, so she was certain to ask her friends for a full report. For a full hour-and-a-half I really 'went to town' and never had I enjoyed talking more or had such an appreciative audience. Those girls were really interested and at question-time I was subjected to a barrage of intelligent enquiries on a variety of topics, ranging from the value of a 'Bullseye' exercise from an aircrew point of view, to the reasons why a Pilot Officer was not always a pilot and how a man who had never even seen inside an aircraft could have the rank of Flying Officer. Several girls wanted to know the meaning of certain words which were typical RAF slang and I kept them amused with explanations of sayings like, 'putting up a black', 'pressing the tit', 'gone for a burton', 'bags of scrambled egg', and 'lobbing down in the drink'. It was only on such occasions that one realised just how much slang there was in normal RAF conversation and how difficult it must have been for other people to understand what we were talking about. In the evening I went along to the camp concert and sat with Dot amongst the boys and girls of the Battery – a solitary blue figure in a field of khaki. It had been a delightful day and I was especially glad to know that Dot had such grand comrades. They were a happy crowd and had something akin to the squadron spirit of the RAF.

The time of my return came all too soon and as the boat pulled slowly out of Belfast harbour, I almost wished that I had never been posted from Aldergrove. Dot and I could have had such glorious times together. But those were typical end-of-leave blues. I had not the slightest desire to return to engine-fitting as a wartime occupation, and as for leaving my wife in NI, well, there had been a very strong rumour that her Battery was to be disbanded and it was quite probable that she would soon be posted back to the mainland.

Before returning to Seighford, I spent an afternoon with my people and was delighted to find them in good health. My screening had been a great relief to them and I felt that they were secretly pleased that I was doing so little flying. In fact, since leaving Kirmington I had been airborne on three occasions only, once on bombing practice with a pupil crew and twice on local flips with 'Chalky' White. The folks realised that I would have to do a second tour of ops but their big hope was that the war would be over before the necessity arose – a rather forlorn hope, I thought.

*   *   *

I had not the slightest idea how I came to lose my little red bead which, since the first ops briefing at Elsham, had been worn as a lucky charm on the lapel of my battledress blouse. After twelve months' service it had chosen to desert its post and I felt vaguely uneasy. I informed Dot of the loss and said that I dare not go back on ops without a lucky bead. She promised to get one and send it along. The boys in the section were sympathetic, they knew the value of these things, and suggested I should 'lift' one from the Intelligence Section but I wanted a replacement to appear in a more dramatic fashion, so in the meantime I preferred to leave my safety in the capable hands of 'Joe', assisted by my silver horseshoe.

My comrade, Geoff, had been posted to Hemswell for conversion to Lancasters before returning to ops for his second tour. I was sorry to see him go, we always got along so well together and had been such great friends, both at work and in leisure moments. In his place, two engineers had been posted from Hixon and I was pleased to welcome Ken McDonnell and Tommy Shaw, both ex-Lancaster types and both very young. 'Mac' had completed a good tour with 12 Squadron, including several trips to the 'Big City' during the Battle of Berlin; that all-out assault on the German capital which had lasted from November 1943 to the middle of March 1944, and was dogged by such consistently foul weather. He was on the Peenemünde raid, a tough trip by all accounts; in the light of a full moon, enemy night-fighters shot down 40 of the 600 aircraft taking part in the attack. He also went to Nuremburg on that terrible night in March '44, when 96 aircraft were reported missing from the operation, a black page in the history of Bomber Command. Mac's account of the op reminded me of the trip to the same city, which I have already described, when we effectively fooled the defences.

Tommy's tour had been cut short by a nasty crash over base on the return from a raid. They were making a circuit of the 'drome when a collision occurred with another aircraft which immediately turned over and crashed into the deck. Tommy's kite caught fire and the skipper had to make an emergency landing before the crew could get to crash stations. Flames enveloped the aircraft as it came to a stand-still and Tommy scrambled out of his side-window on to the starboard mainplane. Noticing that the engines were still running and realising the danger to rescuers, he re-entered the cockpit and shut off the switches and fuel. At the same time he heard the bomb aimer calling for help and, at great risk to himself, Tommy managed to drag his crew-mate to safety via the window. On the ground, a quick check-up proved that the mid-upper gunner was still inside the aircraft, so Tommy grabbed a Mae West and, holding it in front of his face, climbed through the door. Making his way up the fuselage, he forced a passage through a wall of flame to the rear spar, where he found the injured gunner struggling to find a way out. Once again, Tommy dragged his man to safety and only then did he allow himself to be led to the ambulance for removal to hospital. Such an experience could be calculated to shake the toughest of men – Tommy was nineteen years old! I felt that I was going to like both these boys.

For several weeks I had been toying with the idea of applying for a commission and, after a serious talk on the subject with 'Chalky', I finally decided that I would be foolish to delay any longer. Our CO at Kirmington had told us that he was recommending us for commissions but I had decided at the time that I couldn't afford one. 'Chalky', however, assured me that the days of heavy Mess-bills were over and that, with care, it was possible to live almost as cheaply in the Officers' Mess as in the Sergeants' Mess. A commission would be a great advantage to me as an instructor, for I often found myself lecturing to and chivvying-around Wing Commanders, Squadron Leaders and the like. There was also the point that I would be going back for a second tour and I didn't relish the idea of operating again as an NCO; that wasn't my idea of making progress. Having made a decision, I obtained the necessary forms and filled them in. A few days after, I was called for an interview by the Station Commander who, after a very pleasant 'grilling', said that he would be delighted to recommend my commission and that I would be called, at a later date, for an interview with the Group Captain at Hixon.

During the months of April and May, Bomber Command had been laying on large scale attacks on rail targets in France and had also carried out a softening-up process along the entire coast of Northern France, the coast which we all presumed would be the scene for the launching of the 'Second Front'. Raids were carried out with only slight losses and with such consistency that the whole business of bombing by the 'heavies' seemed to have developed into a series of glorified cross-country trips. We ex-Ruhr bashers and Battle of Berlin types were inclined to mock at the ease with which tours were being completed, and recalled the days when every op was a full-scale battle from the moment of take-off and were at pains to point out that our real work was only just beginning where these fellows were turning for home. Still, it was all part of the overall strategy and it was heartening to feel that the old 'chop' days were almost over; that we might never again see those long lists of 'Missing, Believed Killed' in the columns of 'The Aeroplane' or 'Flight'. Many of the recent attacks had been carried out in daylight with complete success. We shuddered to think what would have happened to a daylight effort in 1943; the continent would have been littered with shot-down Lancasters, Halifaxes, Stirlings and Wellingtons.

Since my return from leave in Northern Ireland, Dot had been posted to the Plymouth area and was stationed at a site on Rame Head, near Cawsands Bay. On my next leave I went to Plymouth, as Dot was unable to travel owing to restrictions on troop movements except in the course of duty. In fact, the pre-invasion preparations were so advanced that we operational aircrew types were about the only people able to obtain leave. As I travelled on the ferry-boat to Cawsands, I was staggered by the amount of shipping in Plymouth Sound, and it seemed to me that every other ship was a landing craft. Dot had arranged for us to stay at a pleasant little boarding-house overlooking the bay but on the Sunday night, however, she dashed in with the news that she had been given permission to proceed home on leave. We did some high-speed packing and nipped smartly across to Plymouth – just in time to miss the evening north-bound train. We took the London train and arrived home in time for lunch on the following day. In the first three days of that leave, I spent thirty-three hours in railway compartments!

On my return to Seighford, I was greeted with the grand news that 'Mac' had been awarded the Distinguished Flying Medal, and Tommy, the British Empire Medal; I was delighted. They were both good types and I was sure that they had earned their gongs. 'Mac' and I had become great friends and I found him extremely good company. He was keen on his job and had the happy knack of quickly arousing the interest of the pupils, with his whimsical tales of squadron life. Tommy was of a more retiring nature and it seemed to me that he was still feeling the effects of his crash.

It was about this time that I heard of a very nasty prang over at Hixon. On the return from an exercise, an aircraft had crashed and caught fire. The pilot, a chap named Keeler, had been badly burned on the arms and face but was said to be out of danger; other members of the crew were in bad shape. This risk of fire following a crash landing was a question which had worried me ever since I first saw a Hudson crash in flames at Aldergrove. There was something about fire that just sickened my soul. It seemed to be taken for granted that a multi-engined aircraft would go up in flames. I had seen dozens of kites burned to a cinder, some after crashes which had not appeared to be too violent and it was not a comforting thought that at the end of any trip our aircraft might prove to be our crematorium.

I don't remember when this fire business first began to creep into my dreams but it seemed to go back to that awful night at Aldergrove when our CO, Squadron Leader Chafe-Jones, had been killed in a Hudson which had crashed on take-off. Seconds after the crash, the kite was in flames and by the time we reached the spot the aircraft was absolutely unapproachable. Since that time I had been afflicted by recurrences of fire-dreams and had often wondered if they were a foreboding of my own death. The dreams were never the same: sometimes I would be the victim of a crash in flames and at other times it would be some person with whom I was familiar, but always there was the horrible reality that is typical of a dream, and there was always the certainty of death. During the incidents on my first tour when we had been on fire in the sky, these dreams had been quickly brought to mind but, somehow, I never felt that the time had come. The circumstances just didn't seem to fit the dreams and there was not that queer mental recognition which made one say, 'This has all happened before.'

Despite the dreams, I was thoroughly enjoying my screening period and had many friends on the station. I was still billeted in the same Nissen hut to which I had been shown on my arrival and had several other instructors for company. 'Sully', 'Taff', and 'Geordie', were ex-Middle East 'Wimpy' types and were all wireless operators. Sully and Taff had been through the mill in North Africa; Sully was a Flying Boot Club and Caterpillar man, having walked back from behind the enemy lines after a bale-out; Taff qualified for his Goldfish by having ditched twice; and both had spent some time in prisoner-of-war camps. With one exception, the rest of the lads in the billet were ex-Lancaster types, and many and long were the arguments between the Middle East and home-based factions on the merits of their tours. The exception was 'Bax', a ground staff radio instructor. Bax had been a keen 'pot-holer' before the war and he had a fund of good stories concerning the enthusiasts whose idea of a pleasant week-end was to be lowered on a very long rope down a very deep, damp hole in the Yorkshire Dales or, for that matter, any district which had a good supply of deep, damp holes. A fascinating pastime, no doubt, but one which strengthened my conviction that all Yorkshiremen are slightly mad! As that eminent Lancastrian, the late

Professor John Hilton, once remarked, 'They have never quite got over their misfortune of being born on the wrong side of the Pennines'!

In the section, one day, I was lecturing a class of Canadians and mentioned that our mid-upper gunner in the Bunten crew had hailed from a 'hick-joint' known as Sioux Lookout. Up jumped an enraged 'Cannuck' to inquire, 'Wha' d'ya mean, "hick-joint"?' A boob on my part because this lad also came from Sioux Lookout. In the ensuing conversation, I found that he not only knew Eddie Smith, our gunner, but was a great friend and had actually corresponded with him whilst we were at Elsham.

In this most-publicised of all wars, there had been certain incidents which had socked a news-hungry public right in the ear. Sometimes the news was good, sometimes bad, but in either case the effect was the same, one seemed to stagger under the impact and, strangely enough, expectancy did nothing to soften the blow. After almost five years of war, 'headline' news of yesterday was already becoming part of a misty background, but the historic events stood out in the memory. There was no need to consult files to recall the scuttling of the *Graf Spee*; the retreat from Dunkirk; the German attack on Russia; Pearl Harbour; the sinking of the *Hood*, *Bismark*, *Prince of Wales*, *Repulse* and *Ark Royal*; the fall of Singapore; the 1,000-bomber raid on Cologne; Dieppe, Stalingrad and El Alamein; the dam-bursting episode; the Blitz, and the big raids by Bomber Command. But none of these quite equalled in effect the announcement from 'SHAEF', on 6 June 1944, that the Allied armies had landed on the beaches of Normandy, supported by powerful Naval forces, airborne troops, and air cover of overwhelming superiority. A breach had been thumped in the 'unbreakable' Western Wall and the Dunkirk spectre was crushed underfoot as the invading armies poured through the gap. The day of vengeance was at hand.

The whole world shook with the news but this, above all, was surely Britain's day. For years she had been 'taking it' – now it was her turn to 'dish it out'. Our boys were back on the continent and this time there would be no retreat. Neither were they alone, men of many nations ranged themselves alongside the 'Tommies', all with a score to settle with the Hun and all eager to be in at the kill. The oft-libelled Yanks had, at last, been given the chance to justify their strings of medal ribbons; and from cellars and forest camps the French resistance movement came into the open in response to the call to arms. Overhead, a mighty air fleet, with black-and-white striped wings, shuttled across the Channel to blast the enemy wherever he could be found. Every true Allied heart beat faster with the thrill of pride, for this was D-DAY! Would that Shakespeare had been there to immortalise the grandest day in British history – but Britons were ever the same, and what better than to re-echo the words he put into the mouth of that other invader, Henry V, when with 6,000 men-at-arms and 24,000 archers he set sail from Southampton, over 500 years ago:

'Therefore . . . omit no happy hour
That may give furtherance to our expedition;
For we have now no thought in us but France,
Save those to God . . .'

But even on this day of days there was still the common task to be performed. The engine-fitter had his inspections; the cook, his preparation of the day's meals; aircrew under training must press on with circuits-and-bumps; the store-basher had to repeat his usual cry, 'You'll have to get a chit!'; and the Met. people had to consult their fir-cones and bunions. For myself, however, the day also had a personal significance; I had to report at Hixon for my interview with the Group Captain. It was, I felt, a happy coincidence. Surely, no one – not even a Group Captain – could be hard-hearted on D-Day.

On arrival at Hixon, I renewed acquaintance with Bill Bailey who had also applied for his commission and was, in fact, due for an interview that very day. Bill had little news of the old crew; Reg Boys was still at Whitchurch, Corky was somewhere in Scotland, Eddie had been commissioned and was at a Canadian OTU somewhere in the Midlands, nothing definite was known of Reg Bunten or Doug, except that Reg had been commissioned and had done some dicing at Lindholme. I also called on Leo Flatt, a fellow-engineer, who had already taken his commission and was expecting to be posted back to an operational squadron for a second tour.

I presented myself at the appointed hour to the Station Warrant Officer and, a few minutes later, was shepherded into the *sanctum sanctorum*. The Group Captain had only recently been posted to 30 OTU and this was the first time I had seen him. He was an Australian and I immediately classed him as 'one of the boys' – a thought which did much to dispel my slight feeling of nervousness. I made my salute and, after an exchange of courtesies, the CO asked me if I thought that the policy of using flight engineers at an OTU was a sound one.

77

I stretched myself on this 'gift' question. I was on safe ground and I left 'Groupy' very little time for more searching questions. The interview over, I was rewarded by a smiling assurance that my recommendation would be forwarded to 93 Group Headquarters, and that my next and final step would be an interview with the AOC.

The 6th of June 1944, had indeed been a day to remember.

A month later, I set course along the well-worn route to Stafford railway station, with a leave-pass safely tucked into my tunic pocket. Much as I enjoyed my work in the RAF, I was never slow to seize the opportunity whenever the chance of a spot of leave presented itself. Whilst waiting for my train, I divided my time between drinking cups of tea in the canteen and sauntering along the platform, and it was during a spasm of the latter that I met an acquaintance of Elsham days. Flight Sergeant Steele was a pilot who had been very popular on the old squadron and during our conversation we recalled many happy incidents of those grand times and exchanged news of our mutual friends. Unfortunately, he was unable to give me any gen on the missing crews.

As always happens when one is deeply interested in a conversation, my train came into the station bang-on-time and I had to say 'Goodbye' to 'Steely'. As I journeyed north, my mind, inspired by the meeting, continued the reminiscences. I saw again the unmistakable, beautifully coloured target indicators of red, and the supporting green, dripping slowly into the heart of some German city, and heard Corky's gleeful cry 'There go the reds'! What thrills were bound up in that phrase, it had all the significance of the Battle of Britain boys' 'Tally ho'! Just four little words, but what a host of memories they conjured up. Memories of piercing, blue-white searchlight beams; the pungent smell of close-bursting flak; of the wicked black shapes of night fighters, darting about like fish in the bomber stream; of angry, black columns of smoke rising from battered objectives to a height of 18,000 feet or more; of the uncanny shock-waves radiating from bursting 'cookies'; and the amazing 'scarecrows' put up by the cunning Hun to simulate an exploding aircraft. I could see too, the elaborate dummy firesights which Jerry built in the hope that their glittering white lights would tempt the bombs of attacking aircraft; and the dummy target indicators of red and green which were also meant to deceive but which, to the knowledgeable crews, were very obvious for they never could reproduce the exact colours of our markers. Everything was there in my mind's eye, everything that went to make up the typical target scene. Nor could the incidents of the return trips be forgotten. The dull red glow in the eastern sky which could still be seen as we looked back from the enemy coast; the streaks of tracer on the sea below, which told of battles of the 'little ships'; terrific flashes in the sky as some aircraft had the cruel misfortune to blow up after gaining the safety of the home coast; and the lame ducks circling base with one undercart wheel down and one up. I underwent the sensations of the occasional heavy landing, when Reg, weary after a long, hazardous trip, would bring 'William' down with a heart-sickening thump, and as we progressed down the runway in a series of vicious lurches, Bill would sarcastically chant, 'Landed 04.41 – airborne 04.42 – landed 04.43 – airborne 04.44 – landed 04.45 hours'!

In actual fact, my leave train was just pulling out of Crewe station, but my mind was still back at Elsham and I remembered with a rueful smile, the day when, clad only in swimming trunks, I had fallen to sleep under a blazing sun and had severely burned my skin in sundry places. That night, I flew in a state of acute discomfort, with every movement of my body bringing painful chafing from the straps of my parachute harness. And then there was that time at Kirmington when Eddie and I had been playfully scrapping on the grass before take-off; locked together we fell to the ground and the solid steel clip of my harness, backed by ten stone or so of flight engineer, rammed into Eddie's heart. He lay gasping for breath and every vestige of colour drained from his face. We were scared by the turn of events and sent for the Medical Officer who, inside half-an-hour, had Eddie back on his feet. The gallant Canadian looked very shaky and we tried to persuade him to 'stand down' but, as long as he could swing a turret and squeeze a trigger, he was determined to fly and 'William' took off a few minutes later with his normal crew.

I thought of the ever-present hazards of life on an operational squadron, of kites blowing up on the runway and just at the moment of take-off; even of kites which blew up after a mission or before a mission, when doing nothing but standing peacefully in their dispersal points. The affair of 'C-Charlie' was a typical example. The aircraft stood in dispersal on the night of an operation, bombed up and ready for the preliminary ground-testing of engines and equipment. An hour before take-off, the crew climbed in and were carrying out their checks when warning cries from the ground staff sent them scuttling out again. The bomb load was on the deck and several cans of incendiaries were burning and had set fire to the underside of the fuselage. An SOS was phoned from the Flight Office for a fire-tender, and pilots running engines in nearby dispersals were signalled to taxi their aircraft out of the danger zone. Suddenly, there was a shattering explosion and a blinding sheet of flame shot 500 feet into the air, taking with it the unfortunate 'C-Charlie'. By a miracle, there was only one fatality. A wireless operator, checking his equipment in an aircraft standing several dispersals away, was killed by a lump of metal which had been projected horizontally at high speed.

Having spent a few hours at home with my people, I hurried to Manchester for the midnight train to the West Country. Dot was still at Rame Head and had again arranged for us to stay at 'The Haven', Cawsands.

During the week, we went over to Plymouth and I was horrified to see the amount of bomb damage in the centre of the city. The *Luftwaffe* had really blitzed the famous old port and there was little hope of revisiting the scenes of childhood days when, during the 1914–18 war, I had lived in the town with my mother and my father, who was serving with the Royal Naval SBR. But the *Luftwaffe* could not rob me of memories of days when we would sit on the Hoe and watch the warships in the Sound; of the booming of guns as ships opened-up on practice shoots; or of my great friendship with 'Winky', that lovable American sailor who gave me candy and coloured comics. In those days, the only craft I remembered seeing in the sky were the silvery 'blimps'. The ruins before me testified to the 'progress' made in the intervening years. But even this desolation was not the ultimate in man's destructive power and cunning. On 'D-Day + 7' there had begun the German attack on London by the secret weapon 'V1' or flying bomb, and in spite of constant raids by Bomber Command on the launching sites in the Pas de Calais, they still continued to arrive in large numbers.

Returning once more to Seighford, I found that the staff had been increased by the posting-in of two more engineers, Don Glen and Dick Orchard, both ex-Lancaster types and both good fellows. Don had been an engine fitter in the Maintenance Section at Elsham when I was on my first tour, and it seemed almost impossible that he could have taken his various training courses and completed a tour of ops in the time. But it was so, and it drew my attention to the fact that I had been screened for over eight months and that I could expect to be recalled at an early date for my second tour. There was already news that Leo Flatt had been posted to a Pathfinder squadron at Oakington, as engineer in Wing Commander Coulson's crew, and as we had been screened at about the same time, I felt that my turn could not long be delayed.

On the last day of August, I went to Group Headquarters for my interview with the AOC and returned with the confident feeling that it was 'in the bag'. A fortnight later, my optimism was confirmed by the grand news that my commission was 'through'.

The business of getting 'cleared' as an NCO involved a great deal of chasing around and form-filling, and I felt relieved when I had finally handed in all my kit, with the exception of my flying clothing and the suit of 'best blue' in which I was to travel home. It is never easy to part with personal possessions and I felt a pang of regret as I watched the WAAF in the Main Stores, fling my kit on to the piles of discarded clothing. I was even sorry to part with those long woollen underpants which, for over four years, had never strayed further than the bottom of my kit-bag.

After clearing, I was given seven days' 'kitting-leave' and I hurried home in high glee. With the RAF's sixty-quid voucher in my pocket, I descended on the Service outfitters in Manchester and 'blued' the lot. As the tailor busied himself with measurements, a few Naval and Army officers sauntered by and gave me friendly nods or passed brief remarks about the weather, and I felt a strange glow of pride at their acknowledgement of my new status. I wondered idly what the Aldergrove boys would say if they could see me, trying on an officer's peaked hat for size. How they loved to pull my leg after I had volunteered for aircrew: I was only an LAC at the time but they began to call me 'Sarge' or 'Chiefy'. They thought it great fun – and it was done only in fun – and it did seem, at the time, that I was reaching for the moon. But now my 'Sarge' and 'Chiefy' days were over, and should I chance to meet my former pals of '1405' they would, by rules and regulations, have to greet me with a salute and call me 'Sir'.

I had hoped to spend a few days with Dot, who had recently been posted to a gunsite at Portishead near Bristol, but there were several annoying delays in connection with my uniform and I was unable to make the trip. Very disappointing for both of us.

On arrival at Stafford station on the return from leave, I found myself stranded in the early hours of the morning and, after gripping the peak of my new hat for assurance, I tested out my recently-attained authority by phoning to the 'drome for transport 'For Pilot Officer Ashton'! It worked, and, remembering too many dreary trudges back to camp in the old days, I felt that I had made a good start in my new job.

A few days after settling down to work in the section, I learned that I was going to Lichfield on a 'Junior Officers' Course' and, in spite of my love for Seighford, I felt glad to be going to a new station, if only for a few weeks.

On the following morning, Dick Orchard strolled into the section rather later than usual. He had been waiting to collect the mail from the Mess, and as he walked over he tossed a letter on to the perspex-topped desk. Recognising Dot's handwriting, I opened the envelope at once and, as I did so, a tiny object dropped out. I smiled as I picked up a red, bead-headed pin. Dot had kept her promise to replace the lucky charm I had lost four or five months before. The boys laughed and reminded me that I had wanted the charm to be replaced in a dramatic fashion. After reading the letter, I fixed the pin in the lapel of my battledress and was just testing it for security when a 'runner' from the Orderly Room came into the section and reported that my Lichfield course had been scrubbed and that I had been posted to an operational squadron!

So I was going back on ops again? It was a terrific thrill and I hurried over to HQ to get the full gen. There I found another thrill waiting for me; I was going to 156 Squadron, stationed at Upwood, Huntingdonshire, a squadron of the Pathfinder Force. Whacko! Back to the good old Lancs and a second tour with the 'cream of the cream', the one-and-only PFF. Throughout the whole of my first tour with Main Force, I had an almost reverent regard for the lads who blazed the trail on every major operation and had felt that life could hold no greater reward than to be chosen to fly in that select company. And now I was actually posted to a Pathfinder squadron.

My screening period was over and I could look back on eleven months of really interesting work. I would be sorry to leave the Airmanship Section, which had been so much in my thoughts during the past year and bore so many reminders of my enthusiasm for the work of an Operational Training Unit. Those painted plywood boards round the walls, on which I had so painstakingly printed the various crew drills and engine-handling drills; the dozens of posters which pictorially described every aspect of airmanship; the different types of dinghies which I had laboriously inflated morning after morning; and the scores of items of equipment and engine parts which I had assembled and taken apart so often that I could literally do it blindfolded. Yes, it had all been great fun and I hoped that I had played my part well in the training of the crews. Perhaps I would meet some of them on the new squadron and I would then be able to find out whether my instruction and advice had been of value. I was also going to miss the boys of the section; Chalky, Dick, Mac, Tommy and Don, had all been very good friends and it had been a pleasure to work in their company.

On my last night at Seighford, I stood looking at the pile of flying clothing on my bed and felt really thrilled by the sight of my old flying boots, helmet, white sweater, silk scarf, gloves and all those things that reminded me of ops. Carefully checking each item for serviceability and adjustment, I replaced them in the kit-bag and snapped the lock. I was all set for action. I wondered if my luck would hold out on my second tour. There seemed no reason why it shouldn't; conditions were certain to be better than in 1943. Jerry was steadily being driven back to his own country and a considerable portion of the 'enemy coast' had been cleared, thus robbing him of a valuable part of his early-warning system. Bomber Command raids had been switched back to German targets but the relatively slight losses indicated that the enemy air defences were crumbling slowly. There was reason to believe that Jerry was getting dangerously short of fuel and that before long, his cities would be completely at the mercy of the Allied bombers. I couldn't have cared less, for if any nation invited extinction it was the German nation, which had for so long gloated over the destruction of our own and other cities. All things considered, there was every chance of my continued survival – a point I was rather keen on – and there was still the assurance of my palm-reading Indian friend that I would still be around when the war ended.

My only doubts concerned my own feelings. Had the eleven months' screening and veritable 'grounding' affected my nerve at all? I didn't think it had but that point could only be settled by my first mission. The true nature of 'nerve' was always difficult to define and the subject had formed the basis of many arguments in the old days at Elsham. Corky, especially, had been fond of raising the topic. Also, in conversation with non-aircrew types, I had often been asked the question, 'Were you ever afraid on ops?' and I always found it hard to answer. There had certainly been occasions when I had experienced some alarming sensations, and occasions when I had murmured fervently to myself, 'Let's get to hell out of here!' and yet, at the same time, I would not have changed places with any man. There was something about operational flying that could not be explained, something in the feeling of being apart from the world, of existing only in that familiar half-gloom and hearing always that muffled roar from the engines. Perhaps the finest comment on the subject was one which I read in an RAF publication: 'Innate fear-lessness – the possession of a few only – is not so important an asset in operations as is courage, which is a state of mind in which fear is present but is controlled and mastered for the sake of attaining an object.'

As the train hauled itself out of Stafford station, I gazed through the window of my compartment at the Wellington aircraft which was making preparations to land at Seighford. It was the last link with another chapter in my life, and as the shark-like fin of the 'Wimpy' disappeared behind a clump of trees, I smiled contentedly and settled comfortably into my seat. This was my happy day; why worry about the future? For the present there was the glorious thought that I was going back on ops, as a Pathfinder!

CHAPTER FIVE

WE LIGHT THE WAY

The WAAF driver, who had rescued me from a lengthy term of imprisonment in the draughty, ill-lit booking office at Holme railway station, gave me all the gen as we swept along the rain-sodden roads to Warboys. Apparently, all aircrew postings destined for Upwood, or for any of the Pathfinder squadrons in '8 Group', had first to report to the training unit at Warboys for an operational refresher course and specialised instruction in PFF technique. There were two outfits on the station, flying Lancaster and Mosquito aircraft; and the Lanc. course, for chaps who were not crewed-up, was usually of short duration. All very interesting but why hadn't I been informed of this before I left Seighford? As it was, I had wasted a couple of hours at the telephone, trying to arrange transport to Upwood and then, after finally getting the score, spent a further hour contacting Warboys; a state of affairs rendered more annoying by the fact that I had already missed dinner and would be lucky to make supper!

On the following morning, I was joined by two more 'free-lance' flight engineers who had also been posted to Upwood, and as we were all ex-Lancaster, second-tour types, we struck up an immediate friendship. Frank ('Brooky') Brooks and 'Whizz' Wisby had just completed their screening tours as instructors at Wimpy OTUs, so we had quite a lot in common. Our first job was to complete our arrival-forms and, whilst engaged in this binding occupation, we met my friend of the 'Hercules' engine course, Jock McDonald. Good old Jock! He was still bemoaning his luck and couldn't understand why he, of all people, had been posted to a Pathfinder squadron. He detested Pathfinders! Furthermore, he hadn't a clue on Lancasters; in any case, he hated the darned things! I just chuckled my way through his grumbles; this was the Jock of old and I was delighted to learn that he, too, was Upwood-bound.

In the afternoon, the new arrivals gathered in the large lecture

85

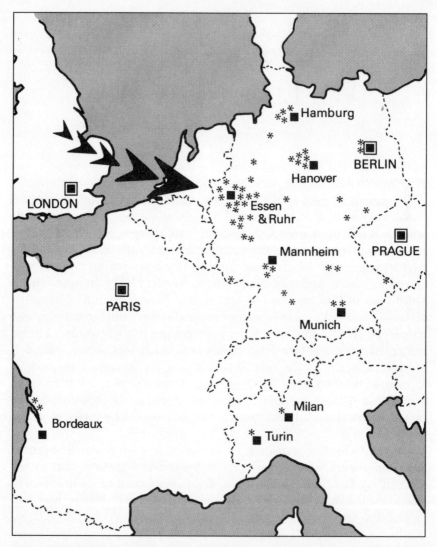

Targets attacked by the author during first and second tours. Most of the raids were directed against the industrial cities of the Rühr Valley

room for an address of welcome by the AOC, Air Vice-Marshal D.C.T. Bennett. This was quite a thrill, for 'Don' Bennett had a terrific reputation, both as a peacetime and wartime pilot, and as the brain behind the Pathfinder Force. He was fast becoming a legend and throughout the Command the PFF squadrons were known as 'Bennett's Air Force'. During his talk, he gave us a brief outline of the formation and growth of PFF, and ended by speaking of the high morale of the crews and the success which invariably attended their efforts.

The course started with a series of lectures for all categories and these proved very interesting and informative. I learned that I would be crewed-up at Upwood and that my tour would consist of twenty-five missions, or more in the event of operating against French targets, which did not earn as many 'points' as German targets. This meant that I would do more dicing than if I had been posted to Main Force, where twenty trips were needed for a second tour. Then followed an explanation of the various types of crews which made up a PFF squadron, together with details of duties performed by each type. The terms 'Visual Markers', 'Supporters', 'Blind Markers', 'Visual Centrers', 'Blind Sky Markers' and 'Illuminators', were some-what puzzling but I figured they would make sense as the course progressed. Some of the code-names used in describing the marking technique were, of course, very familiar and I knew all about the activities of those heroic characters, the 'Master Bomber' and the 'Deputy Master Bomber'. I gathered that in 'Blind' crews the target was marked on instruments by two navigators working as a team and that, in the event of unserviceability, markers were retained and bombing was carried out on the normal bombsight by the flight engineer. In 'Visual' crews, a pukka bomb aimer marked the target by visual identification; and in 'Supporters', who did not drop markers, the bombing was entirely the engineer's pigeon.

To further assist in the explanation of the Pathfinder technique, we were shown a film on the 'H2S' set. This special radar equipment comprised mainly a scanner housed in a streamlined blister on the underside of the aircraft's fuselage, and a viewing-screen and controls, operated by the 'Nav. 2', in the navigators' compartment. By a complicated business of transmitting and receiving radio waves, into which I did not probe too deeply, a progressive map of the territory over which the aircraft was flying was projected on to the viewing-screen, irrespective of the presence of cloud or darkness. Operationally, H2S enabled the Nav. 2 to drop markers and bombs on to an otherwise invisible target – it was, in short, a target-area navigational bombsight.

After the film show, we had a session on the types of flares used by PFF and the method of using them for marking targets under various conditions. During my first tour I had heartily disliked ten/tenths cloud attacks when bombing was done on sky-markers, but after seeing the crafty delay-fuses used and learning of the calculations necessary for their successful use, I cast a more friendly eye on this ingenious method of defeating nature.

Towards the end of question-time, several chaps asked about the Pathfinder Badge – that coveted, winged emblem worn on the flap of the left breast-pocket by qualified aircrew members of PFF squadrons. I was surprised to learn that the badge was not awarded automatically but had to be earned. To qualify, it was first necessary to complete a certain number of operations on which the target was actually marked; with these trips safely in the log-book, the next step was a thorough examination in one's particular trade by the various specialists, and successful candidates gained the Temporary Award of the Pathfinder Badge. On completion of a tour of ops with a Pathfinder squadron, the individual careers were reviewed and, in satisfactory cases, the Permanent Award was made. There was a strict regulation that the badge was not to be worn on battledress nor carried on an operational sortie.

The course for flight engineers was very well organised and I was able to modify my Lancaster gen in the light of new methods which had been incorporated in the various drills since I last operated. We also had another job to learn – bomb aiming. The flight engineer was certainly regarded by PFF as a very versatile member of the crew: he was expected to be a first-class engineer; have the ability to pilot the aircraft in an emergency; be capable of manning any of the gun turrets; act as bomb aimer in certain crews; be able to identify stars and constellations; learn to use the navigator's sextant and be able to take reliable 'shots' with that instrument!

Whilst waiting for the Flight Commander to sign my log-book on my last day at Warboys, I picked up a booklet giving the gen on demobilisation and could not help smiling at the thought of checking up on demob. at a time when I was preparing to embark on another tour. However, for future reference, I jotted down the applicable Bevin Scheme formula – 'Release Group 23'.

On the morning of 25 October 1944, Brooky, Whizz and I piled our kit into Brooky's car, and after a few parting words with Jock, who had to stay another week to complete his conversion from Stirlings to Lancs., set course for Upwood, 156 Squadron, and the unknown future.

Shortly after arriving at Upwood I entered the Ante Room and a mocking cry of 'dinghy dinghy, prepare for ditching!' drew my attention to a group of chaps staring in my direction, and I was delighted to see several ex-Seighford types beckoning to me. As I walked over to them, I recognised 'Ginger' Wallace of the flowing moustache, Kitson, Pelly, and the Canadian Mason, with various members of their crews, conspicuous amongst whom was 'Tubby', Pelly's jovial navigator. Greetings over, I questioned them about their adventures since leaving 30 OTU of life at HCU and at 1 Group squadrons. They had such a lot to tell of their early days with Main Force and were able to give me some interesting information on the activities of some of the other boys who had trained with them. There was one sad item in the news; Geoff Battersby had been killed. Poor Geoff; he was such a good type and we had worked so well together. The boys congratulated me on being commissioned and when they learned that I had joined 156 Squadron, they vied with each other in giving me all the gen on my new outfit. The squadron crest was pointed to with pride and I was suitably impressed by the design, which expressed the purpose of the squadron without having to resort to a Latin tag. Incorporated in the crest was a spirited Mercury, bearing aloft a flaming torch, and the honest-to-goodness motto, 'We Light the Way'. The squadron, it appeared, was peopled entirely by wizard types, and a glance round the Mess seemed to confirm the assertion that there were more 'gongs' per square yard at Upwood than at any other station in Bomber Command – judging by a brief recital of the operational records of some of the gong-bearers, the awards were earned the hard way. Conscious of my solitary ribbon, the 1939–43 Star, I felt that my work during my second tour would have to be very good to justify continued presence in such distinguished company.

In addition to the Lancaster squadron, commanded by Group Captain Bingham-Hall, Upwood also boasted a Pathfinder Mosquito squadron, the 'Jamaica' 139 Squadron, commanded by Wing Commander Voyce, and I gathered that relations between the two outfits were most cordial. The Mosquito boys were just drifting out to briefing and as they passed our group I recognised a chap named Groom, who had been with 103 Squadron; he was an NCO in those

156 Pathfinder Squadron, Upwood

days but had risen, in the intervening period, to the rank of Flight Lieutenant.

Two more ex-Seighford types, Squadron Leader Gilbert and Flight Lieutenant Todd spotted me and were ready to swap '156' gen for my latest news from 30 OTU. They were greatly amused at the story of an incident which had occurred on my last day at Seighford; one of the more-experienced screen pilots had taken up a Wimpy on weather-test and had as his crew, three more screen pilots. On completion of the test, the Wimpy, with its talented if somewhat boisterous crew, was turned into the funnel and began to make the perfect approach to a perfect landing. All four agreed it was going to be a peach of a touchdown and mock congratulations were bandied about on the intercom. As they approached the deck, one intelligent soul did remark that they seemed to be much lower than usual but not until the rasping sound of a fuselage tearing along a runway broke into the conversation, did anyone realise that a perfect belly-landing had been made! The reception by the Commanding Officer was, so rumour had it, decidedly chilly. The remarks of the pupil pilots, concerning their mentors, were worth going a long way to hear!

On my way to the Crew Room for 'Prayers' – as we called morning briefing – I was able to take a quick look at my new station and was delighted with everything I saw. The Mess itself was a lovely building, with garages and playing-fields at the back, car park and tree-lined drive at the side, and tennis courts, standing at a discreet distance from the grass-crescented entrance, at the front. Between the Mess and Station Headquarters there were well-tended flower and vegetable gardens, and a trim little greenhouse which seemed to breathe an air of tranquillity into the otherwise warlike atmosphere. Glancing from left to right as I walked along, I took in the timbered church, the airmen's dining hall – with a distant view of the parade ground, the Sergeants' Mess, post office, Briefing and Intelligence block, assorted buildings belonging to Station Workshops, and finally the huge hangars, without which no RAF station would be complete. Upwood was very easy on the eye, thanks to good design, general tidiness and the presence of many fine trees and grassy patches.

The Crew Room – in contrast to the pre-war, pre-austerity buildings I had just seen – was part of a Nissen block which also housed the Locker Room. Glancing through the open doorway, I saw a forest of chairs, the majority of which were already occupied by the battle-dressed members of the squadron. I cut my way through the fug to a discreet position at the back, from where I could search the assembly for familiar figures and also indulge in a little questioning without incurring displeasure. Shortly after nine o'clock, the CO made his entrance and was loudly cheered by the standing crews, in recognition of his recent promotion from Wing Commander. He took his place amongst the leaders on the platform and continued to smile his appreciation of the welcome whilst the two Flight Commanders called their rolls. The Met. man then produced his charts and gave a summary of the weather; locally for the benefit of people detailed for training trips, and continentally in order to give a pointer to the possibility of an op at night – the outlook was not promising. I was amazed at the extent of the training programme, practically every aircraft was down for either practice bombing or H2S exercises, and I learned from some of the chaps around that the squadron did more training than an OTU. Obviously an overstatement, but it shook me when I thought back to the free-and-easy days at Elsham. The end of the proceedings was signalled by the CO taking his leave, and I sat down to await the religious service. A guarded query to a nearby gunner brought the reply that 'Prayers' was over and he had no idea why it was called 'Prayers', unless it was that people prayed they were not down for training and could sneak back to the Mess for a game of snooker! For several minutes there was a vocal free-for-all and then the crowd began to disperse, crews detailed for flying wandered into the locker room to collect their kit, and the rest of the chaps made their way to the various sections. Feeling rather a lost sheep, I left the crew room. Brooky and Whizz were waiting outside and together we trailed in the wake of some F/E types who led us past a hangar, housing Mosquito aircraft, into another hangar with more 'Mozzies' and a floor littered with drop-tanks, and eventually fetching-up at a green-painted door bearing the strange device, 'FLIGHT ENGINEERS' SECTION. LEADER – F/Lt. BINGHAM'. Strange, because I had never seen an engineers' section worthy of a name-plate nor yet seen a flight-engineer with the exalted rank of Flight Lieutenant.

Bingham gave us a very cheery welcome and introduced us to the other engineers. Apparently, free-lance engineers were at a premium and the warmth of our welcome probably owed something to the fact that our arrival meant there was less chance of chaps having to do 'spare bod' trips – a practice which was universally disliked. Amongst the lads in the section at the time were two commissioned types, Larry Mooney and Syd Clift; and NCOs 'Ginger' Lumb, 'Gaffer' Gedney, 'Jock' Bruce, Frank Wilds and 'Pret' Pretlove; the rest of the boys were on training or on leave. We learned that it was a two-flight squadron and that a certain amount of rivalry existed between the men of 'A' Flight and 'B' Flight, each claiming to have the better crews and aircraft. But there was no difference of opinion on the quality of the squadron and we were soon convinced that '156' was far-and-away the best squadron which ever marked a target. The boys spoke reverently of skippers like Griffin, Letford, Dwen, Cochrane, Clayton, Ison, Robertson and Falconer, and were shocked that we had never heard of them, a state of affairs which we hastily explained away by saying that we had been buried at OTUs for twelve months.

During a lull in the conversation, I raised the question of crewing-up and was informed that the matter would be fixed during the morning, but that we were at liberty to make our own arrangements if we had already contacted a crew needing an engineer. The crew position was rather involved, I gathered, and very different to the system on Main Force, where crews arrived complete and invariably flew together until they were either screened or prematurely eliminated from the battle. On a Pathfinder squadron there were usually a few complete first-tour crews who had graduated from Main Force but the majority were made up of a mixture of second tour, third tour, extended PFF tour, and first tour odd-bod types. A typical crew of this sort might fly together for a few trips and then perhaps the engineer would be screened, next the navigator would be screened, followed shortly afterwards by the rear gunner, each being replaced in turn by a spare bod or a free lance. In the majority of cases, therefore, the crews did not fly together for very many trips and the squadron was essentially of a floating nature.

The engineers had no organised 'tea-swindle' of their own, so at ten o'clock we repaired to the Gunnery Section, and it was in the company of the hawk-eyed fraternity that I heard the story of the Gunnery Leader's toe; an unusual subject to discuss over a cup of char, but one which proved very interesting. The Leader – the gunners informed me – hailed from Southern Ireland and had volunteered for flying duties in the RAF during the early part of the war. Unfortunately, he had a hammer-toe, or some similar disability of the foot, and was turned down by the medical examiners. Nothing daunted, he immediately went into hospital and had the offending toe removed, and after a suitable interval again presented himself for examination. To his disgust, the medicos pointed accusing fingers at the toe-less foot and said, 'Nothing doing, chum'! Now that should have been enough to deter even the most enthusiastic volunteer but that Irishman just pestered and pestered until he was eventually accepted. His subsequent rank of Squadron Leader and the ribbons of the DFC, the GM and the BEM further testified to the spirit of a man from what was, of course, a neutral country. I had no reason to disbelieve the story and felt ashamed to think that many of my own countrymen had exercised similar persistence and ingenuity for the sole purpose of *avoiding* service with the armed forces.

Back in the section, I chatted with 'Gaffer' Gedney, a very likeable Yorkshireman, and learned that he had been badly burned when a Mosquito crashed into the billet in which he had been sleeping. There were several casualties from the crash and the ensuing fire, and 'Gaffer' could have been excused if he had hated the sight of aircraft, but he seemed completely unperturbed. I was always impressed by people who could take bodily punishment without losing courage – it was so easy to be tough and enthusiastic when everything was going smoothly but the real 'guts' only emerged after taking a heavy rap from Fate. It may have been that my own keenness would be somewhat dulled by physical injury but, so far, it had not been tested – the indications were that my second tour might supply the answer, to expect another trouble-free tour was almost an impertinent thought.

I was in the Ante Room, dividing my attention between a cup of coffee, a cigarette and the daily paper on the one hand, and a running conversation with Brooky on the other, when Bingham came across to inform me that I had been crewed up with Flight Lieutenant Todd. The news was very acceptable, for at Hixon and Seighford 'Toddy' had a good reputation, both as a pilot and as a sociable type. As I chatted with Bingham, my new skipper walked over and I could tell from his expression that he was quite satisfied with the arrangement. After Bingham had drifted away, Toddy and I strolled round the Mess and I was introduced to the other members of the crew as we located them. There was Flight Lieutenant 'Jacko' Jackson, the rear gunner, a second tour type who had spent some considerable time at Central Gunnery School and was evidently something of a gen-man; the navigational team consisted of Flight Lieutenants Allan Ewens and Lauran Farris, Australian 'box-basher' Nav. 2, and Canadian Nav. 1, respectively; Flying Officer Andy Watson, the second tour wireless operator, was on leave at the time, but I met 'Paddy' Dillon who was deputising during Andy's absence; the remaining member of the crew was the mid-upper gunner, Flight Sgt Denis Price, and I would probably meet him during the afternoon.

I was immediately impressed by the maturity of the crew: I was thirty-two years of age and it was quite evident that at least three of the others were even older. At a rough estimate, I put the average age of the crew at over thirty – rather remarkable in a game which was usually considered to be a young man's province. During the conversation, I asked about the previous engineer and learned that he had been a victim of one of those ghastly accidents which are always liable to happen on an operational 'drome. A kite was being de-bombed after a trip, when a terrific explosion made a shambles of the aircraft and the dispersal point. Several ground staff lads were killed or badly injured and Toddy's engineer lost a leg. There was something sickening and dispiriting about this type of accident – one felt that it should never have happened.

Toddy was a comparative newcomer to the European theatre of operations, as his first tour was completed on Wimpys in North Africa and Malta. He had taken over Wing Commander Scott's crew and,

Crew of L-London: left to right, 'Jacko' Jackson (rear gunner), Allan Ewens (navigator 2), Andy Watson (wireless operator), Lauran Farris (navigator 1)

having already done eight trips with them, would fly with them for thirteen more, after which the navigators were due for screening; four trips after that, Toddy himself would have finished; thus, I would be left with eight trips to do with another skipper. All very confusing. The crew was a 'Blind Sky Marker' outfit, and our job was to drop the flares used for marking a target when cloud made identification of ground markers difficult or impossible. We did not carry a 'straight' bomb aimer. I learned that we were a 'B' Flight crew, that our aircraft 'L-London' was comparatively new and dead reliable, and that the ground crew was efficient and enthusiastic. There was one other item of news that was not to be scorned, we were due to go on leave in a week's time!

Next day, I signed-out a kit of tools and a torch from the squadron stores, collected a parachute, harness and Mae West from the 'chute section, and took them with my flying kit to the locker room. At Upwood, all flying clothing was hung on steel-framed racks in a steam-piped room, and each crew had a particular section for its equipment. This, I thought, was a much better scheme than the one where kit was handed over a counter by attendants. After dumping my stuff, I went out to have a look at 'L-London' and have a chat with the ground crew, after which I installed my mascot 'Joe' in his usual position; the safety and success of aircraft and crew was now assured.

Back at the section, I found that Brooky had been crewed-up with Squadron Leader Nicholls, an Australian ex-Coastal Command type, and Whizz had thrown in his lot with Flying Officer Cann. There was also a surprise waiting for me; two of my friends, Bert Radford and Fred Jenner, both of whom had been commissioned since I met them on the 'Hercules' course, had been posted to the squadron. They had still to do their course at Warboys and were pleased to know that they would be meeting Jock again. It was rather remarkable that of the small number of engineers on the course at Bristol, we four should be posted to the same squadron at the same time.

Whilst strolling down to 'Prayers' with Toddy and the boys, I heard the drone of aero engines and, glancing westward, saw the Fortresses of the American 8th Air Force circling and picking up formation, prior to setting course on a daylight raid. The metalled fuselage and wings of each 'ship', untrammelled by camouflage dope, shone brightly in the rays of the early morning sun, and presented a pretty picture against the background of clear, blue sky. Occasionally, a brilliant red or green Very light was pooped off and this added further colour to the proceedings. It was the first time I had seen the 'Forts' going out on a mission and I was suitably impressed.

Down at the crew room, one only needed to look at the CO's face to realise that his brief-case carried something more exciting than a training programme. I glanced quizzically at Toddy, who smiled and raised a thumb. The Flight Commanders made short work of their roll calls and then the CO selected the all-important sheet from his case and rose to face his audience. Sure enough, it was an op, a 'daylight', and the buzz of whispering increased as the CO waded steadily through the battle-order. My heart missed a beat when he came to 'Todd, in "London"'. We were 'on'!

The word 'Cologne', written in green ink in my log book, testified to the successful outcome of my first daylight raid, and as I flicked over the pages of the book and saw the red-inked entries of night ops in 'William', I decided that 'daylights' were, comparatively speaking, 'a piece of cake'. Everything seemed so easy in the broad light of day; no pre-flight checks with feeble-rayed torch, no stumbling about the aircraft in pitch darkness, no grim lonely stooges to and from the target, no searchlights probing the sky like a dentist searching for a bad tooth, and no struggling to fight off the effects of fatigue during the early morning hours. In daylight, the severe buffetings occasioned by hitting the slipstream of aircraft, were plainly of no consequence and in no way gave the impression of a collision, an all-too-frequent feeling on night ops. Even the flak over the target area seemed quite friendly, for the grey-black puffs of smoke were ridiculous when compared with the angry flashes to which I had been accustomed. Perhaps most of all, I missed the glowing stubs and flaming exhausts of the Merlins; there was always something exciting and comforting about those outward signs of hidden power. There was one particular incident of the trip which impressed me rather forcibly. On the way to the target, our navigators found that we were rather early and Toddy decided to do a 'dog leg' in order to lose a bit of time. At the completion of the manoeuvre, he turned to get back on to course and at that moment Main Force came charging along, literally out of the blue. It was an appalling sight. Seven or eight hundred aircraft bore down on us like a vast swarm of bees; the confounded things were all over the place and we must have bagged a record number of near-misses before finally straightening out. On reflection, I was sobered by thoughts of the number of times the old Bunten crew had orbited targets and done time-losing legs during our tour. We had known full well that the area was infested with aircraft

but 'out-of-sight' was blissfully 'out-of-mind' and phenomenal avoid-
ances had been few and far between. It seemed queer that one had
to do a daylight before one could fully appreciate the enormous risks
of a night operation.

On the morning of my first leave from Upwood, I had the misfortune to be 'Joed' for a training trip. Toddy and the boys had already
set course for Peterborough station whilst I, like a clot, called round
at the section to say 'Cheerio' to the blokes. As soon as I poked my
head through the doorway, old Bingham leapt from his chair and,
before I had time to size up the situation and beat a hasty retreat, he
had grabbed my tunic with one hand and the telephone with the
other. In a brace of shakes, he had fixed me to fly with Flight
Lieutenant Letford and airily waved aside my pleas of a previous
engagement. Tough luck, but I couldn't really grumble – the
squadron was still short of engineers and I had heard so much about
Ken Letford that I was keen to have a flip with him and his much-
vaunted 'A-Abel'.

As we careered round the peri-track in the crew-coach, I
explained to Ken that I was trying to get away on leave and he
promised to clip the corners and have me on my way before lunch.
During the trip, I learned that Ken had been operating since the
early days of the war and that during a tour with Main Force in 1943,
he had done a trip to Berlin with Wynford Vaughan Thomas, the
BBC war correspondent, whose impressions of the trip were
recorded during the flight. The recording was absolutely bang-on
and was broadcast several times. I remembered hearing it in the
Sergeants' Mess at Elsham and I asked Ken about the incident in the
target area which had given rise to a loud cry of 'Line!' from our
boys. He assured me that the rear gunner had actually shot down a
fighter just as they were making their bombing run, and that everything else in the broadcast was quite genuine. The language was
naturally more restrained than usual, but Ken failed to repress his
feelings when the fighter was destroyed. Strangely enough, that slip
of the tongue became quite famous, for on many occasions when
asking civilians if they had heard the broadcast, I was answered by
an enthusiastic 'Rather! Wasn't that the one in which the pilot said,
"Bloody good show!"?' Shortly after that trip, Ken was presented
with a recording by the BBC.

True to his word, Ken had me back at base in good time and,
steering well clear of the section, I nipped smartly into the Mess to
change and then made my getaway – with the solemn resolve that

future mornings-of-leave would be marked by a strict avoidance of Bingham!

Scrubs were exasperating, to say the least, and I had a full share of them during the ten days following my return from leave. To the public, it would appear that Bomber Command was taking a rest but that was far from the truth; in fact, most chaps considered that a series of scrubs was tougher on the system than carrying out the actual missions. Admittedly there had been occasions when a last-minute scrub had brought a sigh of relief but generally there was a sense of frustration.

When I did finally get cracking on the continuation of my tour, it was in a rather spectacular manner – at least, I thought so. The Squadron CO was doing a Master Bomber trip and decided to take over Toddy's crew and kite. The Gunnery Leader was brought in as mid-upper gunner and the Bombing Leader was doing the visual bombing. Quite a glamour crew! A Group Captain, two Squadron Leaders, three Flight Lieutenants, a Flying Officer and a Pilot Officer. But rank meant very little in the air and the daylight op on Münster was very enjoyable. Bingham-Hall was a wizard type and I thoroughly enjoyed flying with him. Like my old skipper, Reg Bunten, he communicated with me by 'signs and wonders' and I soon fell in with his particular brand of signals. A twiddle of the fingers for more revs, an inclination of the hand for climbing power, the droopy thumb for cruising power, and all the old signs so beloved by the enthusiastic type of flight engineer. Whilst we were orbiting the target, Jacko reported that a small object had whizzed past his turret; he volunteered the information that it looked like an exhaust-stub. Bingham-Hall asked if the loss would affect the engine and I assured him that everything would be OK – I had lost stubs before without incurring damage. I had also had an engine wrecked through stub-trouble but there seemed no need to panic on that account; in any case, Jacko was probably mistaken. The return from the trip was uneventful. When the engine blokes checked over the motors in dispersal, they found that the outboard side of the starboard-outer had only five stubs instead of the regulation six. Jacko certainly had a wizard pair of eyes!

Somehow, the daylight ops were leaving me dissatisfied and I began to yearn for the old days. I missed the grimness of the night trips and I missed the solid feeling of flying and living with the same crew. For although I had only been with the squadron for three weeks, I had already flown with five different pilots and, consequently, was not getting to know my own crew as well as I ought to have done.

However, there came a change in the tactics of the 'heavies' and our next seven missions were carried out under the old conditions of blazing targets, dazzling searchlights and the whole familiar kaleidoscope of the terror-by-night. I revelled in the attacks and, on three in particular, positively gloated. Throughout the whole of my first tour – indeed, ever since I started my aircrew training – I had been eager to take part in an attack on Essen. It was such a legitimate target and probably the greatest prize in the whole of the Ruhr Valley. Time and time again had Bunten and crew been briefed for the trip, but never were we able to beat the scrubs which seemed to haunt our attempts to set the seal on our reputations as pukka, dyed-in-the-wool 'Ruhr Bashers'. Little wonder, then, that I enjoyed my two visits to that city with Toddy. And the other attack which gave delight was the fulfilment of a long-anticipated hate-session. On many of our previous runs across North Germany in 'W-for-William', we had been more than annoyed by the vicious nature of that interfering town Osnabrück. When going about our lawful occasions, *en route* for Hanover, Leipzig, Berlin, or such similar destination, we would be set upon by searchlights and flak batteries as soon as the busybodies of Osnabrück got warning of our approach. Now we didn't mind antagonism from the target defences and were quite prepared to play ball with night fighters, but there was something mean-spirited about that half-way house of resistance and we longed for the time when we could devote a whole evening to expressing our displeasure. The score was settled in 'L-London'.

The remaining four of the seven night trips were not without interest, and the names of Coblenz, Duisburg, Soest and Ulm were all newcomers to my log-book. But the period was chiefly made momentous by the advent of an unknown gentleman whose conglomeration of kit I found littered on the floor of my room, on my early-morning return from one of these night sorties. His tunic bore witness to the trade of pilot and rank of Flying Officer but these were the only clues to the identity of the person whose anonymous snores reverberated from the second bed in the room. Snores which gave assurance that they issued from a man who had come to stay.

I liked Freddy Keeler right from the start and he, in turn, seemed quite pleased to make my acquaintance. On comparing notes, we found that we had both been at 30 OTU, he as pupil pilot and I as instructor. It was extremely interesting to learn that he was the Keeler who had been badly burned when his aircraft caught fire after a prang at Hixon. I well remembered the incident for it had made a big impression on me at the time, and I had quoted it in my lectures as an example of what could happen on even the most straightforward of trips. Fortunately, Freddy had made a fine recovery in hospital and all that remained to remind him – physically – of the accident, were the tell-tale bands of shiny skin around his wrists. These marks were a direct result of the almost universal practice of wearing chamois gloves instead of the leather gauntleted gloves so wisely provided by the ever-thoughtful RAF. Other members of the crew were not so fortunate and when Freddy was discharged from hospital, he took over a fresh crew and, on completion of OTU and HCU training, was posted to a Lancaster squadron of 1 Group. After a few sorties with Main Force, he was recommended for PFF and had just finished his course at Warboys.

It was natural that our talk should turn to our lives in pre-Airworks days and the easy flow of confidences pointed to a certain affinity of outlook, and I had the feeling that I had made a great friend.

With nine ops to my credit, I began to feel that I really belonged to the squadron and could converse freely with the stalwarts of '156' without the sensation of addressing superior beings only slightly removed from the gods. Upwood was becoming a real home-from-home for me and was the best station on which I had ever served. The Engineers' Section was also becoming a homely spot. In addition to Brooky, Whizz and the others, we had Jock McDonald, Fred Jenner and Rad Radford, and were further strengthened by the arrival of Freddy Parr and 'Vic' Vickers. Freddy was a member of an Aussie crew skippered by Evans, and he soon became noted for his sparkling wit and unfailing good humour. The only snag was that he was ever reminding people that the 'chop' was just around the corner and Jock, who roomed with him, alleged that their billet floor was littered with old cigarette packets, match boxes and odd scraps of paper which hadn't to be moved, 'in case we get the chop!' Freddy went so far as to compile a 'chop list' with an order of priorities; but some of the more sensitive lads took a very dim view and, by common consent, the offending list was removed. It was inevitable that Freddy should collect the whimsical nickname 'Chop' Parr.

A grand feature of the station was the sunray equipment and whenever circumstances permitted, Whizz and I ambled down to the

KEY TO *Fig. 1*

INSTRUMENT PANEL

1. Instrument flying panel.
2. D.F. Indicator.
3. Landing light switches.
4. Undercarriage indicator switch.
5. D.R. compass repeater.
6. D. R. compass deviation card holder.
7. Ignition switches.
8. Boost gauges.
9. R.p.m. indicators.
10. Booster coil switch.
11. Slow-running cut-out switches.
12. I.F.F. detonator buttons.
13. I.F.F. switch.
14. Engine starter switches.
15. Bomb containers jettison button.
16. Bomb jettison control.
17. Vacuum change-over cock.
18. Oxygen regulator.
19. Feathering buttons.
20. Triple pressure gauge.
21. Signalling switchbox (identification lamps).
22. Fire-extinguisher pushbuttons.
23. Suction gauge.
24. Starboard master engine cocks.
25. Supercharger gear change control panel.
26. Flaps position indicator.
27. Flaps position indicator switch.
28. Throttle levers.
29. Propeller speed control levers.
30. Port master engine cocks.
31. Rudder pedal.
32. Boost control cut-out.
33. Signalling switchbox (recognition lights).
34. Identification lights colour selector switches.
35. D.R. compass switches.
36. Auto controls steering lever.
37. P.-4. compass deviation card holder.
38. P.4 compass.
39. Undercarriage position indicator.
40. A.S.I. correction card hold.
41. Beam approach indicator.
42. Watch holder.

Avro Lancaster instrument panel

medical block and soaked our bodies in the artificial sunlight. A great guy, old Whizz, and we got on famously together. He was collecting ops at an amazing rate, mainly by virtue of the early-morning raids which were being laid-on to help the Army types. On one of these efforts, the sea-wall was breached at Westkapelle, on Walcheren Island, and the widespread flooding forced the enemy to abandon his gun batteries which were barring the use of the port of Antwerp.

Number 156 was a hard working squadron, and this applied to the ground crews as well as the aircrews. The bomb-armourers, I thought were just about the busiest people on the station. Out on the 'drome it was a normal sight to see these lads bombing-up for an op, changing a bomb-load for a revised attack, or de-bombing for a training trip. Winching-up those big, ugly bombs was not easy work and could be highly dangerous. For the bomb-armourer, there was bags of sweat and the ever-present knowledge that any mistake he made might be his last one. Most of the lads seemed to acquire a taste for bombs but I detested the things and never felt really happy until they were safely off the racks. And I failed to see the fun in sitting on bombs as a setting for photographs; the things were lethal at all times, as far as I was concerned, and smug talk about 'safe' bombs didn't win me over. I had learned a very early lesson at Aldergrove whilst watching a burning Hudson which had crashed on take-off. A self-confident Armament Officer had informed me that the depth-charges in the bomb-bay of the kite would not explode, as this could only be brought about by underwater pressure. Having watched the aircraft burn merrily for some time, I had decided to leave and crossed the runway at a reasonable distance from the flames and flying bullets. And then the 'impossible' had happened. With a terrific roar, the Hudson blew up and I had instinctively thrown myself on the ground as great lumps of metal flashed past at high speed. When I had judged that the Hudson had been safely dispersed, I had stood up to see what the score was, and had been somewhat surprised to find a hole in the runway large enough to hold a fair-sized house. Of the aircraft there had been little to be seen; one Cyclone engine, less prop, had been hurled several hundred yards, whilst the rest of the kite had been spread fairly evenly over the 'drome. Windows in hangar offices and cookhouse had been shattered by the blast at a range of about a mile. So when chaps said to me, 'Don't panic, they can't go off!', I usually smiled and moved away; I had heard those words before.

But pleasant and interesting as life was at Upwood, I still felt there was no place like my real home, and had no hesitation in accepting the offer of Christmas leave. It was the first Christmas I had spent with my people since joining the Service and that, alone, was excuse enough for jubilation. But that was not all, for Dot had also wangled leave, as had Bert, my brother-in-law, and the inimitable 'Grindlestone' Green. A real gathering of the clans, and what an orgy of line-shooting. Bert had recently returned from Algiers and was figuratively shaking the sand of North Africa from his boots on to the family hearth-rug; Dot had first-hand experience to relate of the new-fangled flying bombs; and Jimmy weighed in with stories culled from his memories of the Gold Coast and pre-Dunkirk France, and of the work of his unit amongst the wounded who had been evacuated from the Normandy beaches after D-Day.

My contribution to the conversation consisted of a few tales on the lighter side of squadron life. Of the day when Freddy Keeler returned to our room to find that the CO's dog had been sleeping on his bed – the mud from the brute's paws was not the worst of the havoc created, and it was fortunate that the misguided animal had beaten an early retreat. As Freddy was quick to point out, I wouldn't have laughed quite so loudly if it had been my bed. Then there was the affair of Ginger Wallace's pig. Apparently, some enterprising farmer had convinced Ginger that a pig could make a perfect pet, and a deal was clinched over a tankard of ale in the local tavern. The new owner lost no time in boasting of his purchase to a delighted Mess and as the story went the rounds it had lost nothing in the telling. Someone had heard that Ginger had been burning the midnight oil in close scrutiny of *King's Rules & Regulations* to see if there was any just impediment why he should not keep the animal on the station; there were those who claimed that they had actually seen the pig in the car with Ginger, and others who had seen it tethered outside the Mess; but after three pig-less days, it became apparent that Ginger had pulled another of his gags. There was more substance in the tales of 'Shorty' Harris's fire; of the dim type who had never realised that a mouth-wash wasn't meant to be swallowed; and of the pitched battle between two teams of 'screwballs' armed with fire-extinguishers; victors and vanquished had later joined forces for a communal washing of uniforms in the bathrooms. My favourite story, however, was of a more serious nature – at least, it should have been serious but it would have been considered 'bad form' by the hero of the story. Warrant Officer Wright, DFM, was a rear gunner and, apart from a slight limp, there was nothing to distinguish him from the other gunners on the squadron. He had the same happy-go-lucky manner and was ready to take part in anything that was going – even snow-shifting. He was accepted as a normal aircrew type and that was how he liked it. But that was hardly true, for Warrant Officer Wright carried out his duties only by the aid of an artificial leg. There was neither bravado nor false modesty in his attitude, for few heard of his disability at first-hand; and to those in the know, he would make light of the whole affair by such remarks as, 'I mustn't forget to polish up the old leg, I'm on day-off tomorrow!' and 'You should have seen that new bloke's face when I whipped my leg off and used it to knock a piece of wood into the ground!' A gallant gentleman, was 'Wrighty', and I was proud to have met him.

There was a general feeling in our little home-circle that we were celebrating the last Christmas of the war, and there was every reason for confidence. On land, sea and in the air, the Allies were proving too powerful for the enemy and most people realised that complete victory was within our grasp. There was still a lot of grim fighting ahead and it was inevitable that thousands of lives would be lost before the Germans and the Japs were beaten to their knees.

The turn of the year brought a reminder to the squadron that the Reaper was no respecter of persons. Our new CO, Wing Commander Falconer, was killed after a night operation, and the crews of Evans and Pelly failed to return. We of the Engineers' Section were particularly sorry to lose Bingham (with Falconer) and Freddy Parr (with Evans). We remembered Freddy's 'Chop List' and recalled that he had placed his own name at the head. Command of the squadron went to Wing Commander 'Tiny' Ison, and the loss of Bingham brought Brooky the position of Flight Engineer Leader and the rank of Flight Lieutenant. Frank was warned by the boys that leaders on '156' never walked out alive but this only gave him the opportunity to air the latest RAF catch-phrase, 'I couldn't care less'!

And then there came the change in our crew. With trips to Coblenz, Nuremberg, Royan, Hanover and Munich – all crowded into ten days – our navigators, Lauran and Allan, completed their PFF double-tour and, as they had decided to take their screening, we were given a fresh nav. team. Warrant Officer 'Tiny' Walters and Flight Sergeant George Kay were capable types and after a few training trips to mould the new crew, we took them to Chemnitz. Hitherto, most Bomber Command raids had centred on some legitimate target which was conveniently situated in a built-up area, but the attack on Chemnitz – I felt – came into an entirely different category. The

German state was being squeezed from East and West, and the inhabitants of the large cities in the north were panicking down the corridor thus formed to the safety of the 'Southern Redoubt'. The main thought was to get away from the Russians who were rolling steadily towards Berlin, and on this particular night Chemnitz was hanging out the 'House Full' notices. Our purpose, it seemed to me, was to help sort out the overcrowding – the target was well-and-truly plastered and the slaughter must have been terrific. But such was the spirit of the times that in the full knowledge of the crematorium we were leaving behind, Toddy and company were jubilant at the success of their new nav. team. As the blood-red glow receded from

Bombs away over Gelsenkirchen – a 4,000lb 'cookie' accompanied by target indicators

view, thoughts turned to the all-important subject of bacon-and-eggs, and 'London' was whipped-up for a fast crossing of the North Sea. In the grey light of dawn, the boys of '156' waded into their operational breakfast; in far-away Chemnitz, Death stalked through the gutted buildings and claimed his latest recruits.

Toddy's last two trips were to Wesel and Dortmund, and the latter attack enabled me to settle yet another old score. The first trip of my first tour should have been to Dortmund but we had trouble with the flying instruments and had to abandon the mission. Ever since that night, I had longed to retrieve the honour of the crew by visiting that particular spot in 'Happy Valley' but had to do forty-seven trips before I got the chance.

With the completion of Toddy's second tour and the break-up of the crew, came the end of my first phase at Upwood. I had done eighteen trips towards my twenty-five and, as I was putting in quite a lot of work in the section, I decided to complete my tour as a free-lance. In addition to deputising for Brooky at conferences, briefings and interrogations, I had been appointed Air/Sea Rescue Officer for the squadron and station, and was in the throes of organising an ASR Section. I had been awarded the Pathfinder Badge and had been promoted to Flying Officer (with a satisfying rise in pay), so that on the whole I was feeling pleased with life. The friendship with Freddy Keeler had ripened and we spent a great deal of time together. I never tired of his company and it was my secret wish that I could join his crew; but he had a grand engineer in young Joe Moisey and I had to be content with the memory of the single flip I had with Freddy when he and I ferried a kite over from Wyton. Neither of us was over-fond of going out of camp and we usually spent our evenings playing snooker, listening to the radio, writing letters or discussing our private lives. Often enough, the talk was on aircraft and flying in general, for Freddy was always trying to learn just that little bit more about his job. One evening the subject was engine trouble and airscrew feathering, and I passed on gen learned on two and three-engined returns in 'William'. Strangely enough, the Keeler battle-wagon 'K-King' was in trouble after take-off on the night following our discussion, and Freddy had the doubtful satisfaction of feathering a prop. and completing the mission on three engines. It was, in fact, a real press-on effort. But that was not the end of the coincidence, for on the next trip – to Pforzheim – Freddy again had to feather and after staggering round the route in the wake of the main stream, bombed the target on his own from a low altitude. The CO was delighted with the performance of the 'K-King' outfit but reminded them that their luck *could* be pushed too far. After a third feathering trip, it was inevitable that my pal should collect the nickname 'Three-engine' Keeler.

A few days later, the news came through that an immediate award of the Distinguished Flying Cross had been made to Flight Lieutenant Keeler. I was overjoyed, for this was a well-deserved honour. Any clot could make a return trip on three or even two engines when there was nothing to lose and all to gain, but to set out on a long trip – with full tanks and a bomb load – with the knowledge that one would be arriving over the target when all the rest had fled, called for deter-mination of a very high order. To repeat the performance was a wizard show and when the Mess Tannoy blared its invitation for 'the members of 156 Squadron to join Flight Lieutenant Keeler, DFC, at the bar', the boys showed their appreciation in no uncertain manner.

But joy and sadness were ever-present companions in those days and hardly had the thrill of Freddy's gong subsided, when I was staggered by the news that my friend 'Whizz' had failed to return from a night trip. Dear old Whizz, he was such a grand fellow. I did not stay in the section to see his name rubbed off the crew-state board but wandered instead to the medical block for my usual dose of sunray treatment. In the changing room, I suddenly realised that half the fun of the previous visits had been due to the merry companion-ship of Whizz and, without the music of his deep chuckle and the sight of him flicking back his long, blond hair, the whole thing seemed pretty pointless. I decided to scrub round the treatment and returned to the Mess.

In the month that followed Toddy's screening, I did very little flying and my only op was with Squadron Leader 'Willy' Wilson, to Kamen on a daylight effort. Wilson was a religious type and such was the sincerity of his views and general behaviour, that he held the respect and even the admiration of most of the boys. He never used bad language himself and would not permit its use by the crew whilst flying. He was the only man I had ever met on ops who had the guts to read a few verses from his Testament whilst waiting for the crew-coach or for take-off. I found his attitude similar to that of Corky and, as with Corky, I could not quite understand how those views could be reconciled with the business of bombing. The rear gunner in the crew was that grand type, Warrant Officer Wright, and I was honoured to have flown in his company.

In view of my temporary 'chairborne' existence, I was able to take a greater interest in the general life of the squadron, and had a breathing space in which to compare my second tour trips with those of the first, and to review the war as a whole.

The set-up of the squadron had changed considerably, for there had been a great deal of screening, posting and general shuffling around. Our CO, Tiny Ison, had departed and his place was taken by Wing Commander A.J.L. Craig, DSO, DFC, a newcomer to the squadron. Master Bombers Ken Letford and Peter Clayton (both Squadron Leaders with DSO, DFC) were now in charge of 'A' and 'B' Flights respectively, and amongst the crews there had been many old stalwarts posted and an influx of new bods to take their places. Of the engineers who had been with me during my early days in the section, very few remained. Some, like Larry Mooney, Freddy Parr, old Bingham and Whizz, had flown their last mission; whilst a great many more, including Jock McDonald, Freddy Walton, Paddy Hicks and Ginger Lumb, had been posted or were still on the station waiting to be posted. Of the newer crews, there had been a few who had trained at Seighford and I had been particularly pleased to welcome the crews of Jack Cornelius (surely one of the heftiest pilots who ever squeezed into a Lanc. cockpit), 'Benny' Benson (who was always coy on the subject of his age), and pleasant, unassuming George Hampson. It was rather sad that all three should be concerned in incidents which resulted in wounds to crew members, the circumstances of which, however, made me prouder than ever to call them my friends.

George Hampson had flown only a few sorties with the squadron when he ran into his spot of trouble but his handling of the situation was worthy of a veteran. After being attacked by a night fighter, George checked up on his crew and received 'OK' reports from all the boys; he was just congratulating himself on his luck when a series of violent shudders sent the aircraft out of control. George gave an 'Abandon aircraft' order to the crew as he fought to regain control, everybody acknowledged and two of the lads baled out. Shortly after giving the order, George was able to bring the kite back on to an even keel and, after cancelling the order, asked the crew to help him check up on the damage; he had only two replies to his appeal. In addition to the chaps who had baled out, it was found that the mid-upper gunner must have left his turret and fallen straight through a great, gaping hole in the fuselage floor – his parachute was still in position on the fuselage wall. Down in the nose of the aircraft, Bowers – the engineer – was hanging half-way out of the parachute exit and when he was dragged inside it was discovered that his leg had been practically severed by a burst of cannon shells. George brought his crippled aircraft and depleted crew home in masterly fashion and made an emergency crash-landing at Manston. Bowers, who had also been hit in the first attack but had preferred to keep that knowledge to himself until he had finally bombed, was fully conscious the whole time and even applied the tourniquet himself and directed the dressing of the wound. Furthermore, he kept his pilot informed of the state of the serviceable engines. After landing, the engineer was rushed off to the operating theatre and his leg was amputated. George was later awarded the DFC for his part in the night's work and the gallant Bowers received the British Empire Medal.

Flying Officer Benson and crew also met up with a fighter and were hit by shells which wounded the navigators and the wireless operator, knocked out the navigational equipment and most of the flying instruments, and damaged the aircraft in sundry other places. By the aid of much improvisation and ingenuity, Benny – assisted by the wounded crew members – was able to bring the kite back to base. Shortly after this trip, Benny was given replacement crew members and he went out on a mission from which he did not return. I was very sorry, for I had always found Benny to be a decent type; his engineer, 'Woolly' Wolstenholme, had been a great favourite in the section and his loss was all the more tragic because it was only on the previous day that his wife had come to the local village to stay with him for a few days. On the following morning, we learned that Flying Officer Benson had been awarded the DFC for his previous press-on effort.

The third of the trio, Jack 'Corny' Cornelius was stooging home from a raid when a fighter appeared from nowhere and loosed-off a short burst. One cannon-shell found Corny's leg and another tore a neat hole in the sleeve of the engineer's battle-blouse. Corny's wound was rather severe, so he was hauled out of his seat for treatment and the engineer, Bob English, flew the aircraft back to base where the pilot, in spite of his damaged leg, returned to his seat for the landing. Corny collected a well-earned gong – which was sewn-on with the stripes running the wrong way and, crutches or no crutches, he was promptly stung for drinks round the Mess!

These incidents were typical of the spirit of the squadron and an indication of the determination of crews to uphold the prestige of the Pathfinder Force. Even so, we had our boobs. As, for instance, when an experienced crew found themselves coming out over the Dutch coast when they should have been somewhere over Germany! There was also the occasion when a very famous crew was taking off on ops and the pilot – as if to urge his heavily-laden aircraft off the deck – murmured 'Up! Up!' and the engineer, a recent addition to the crew, misinterpreted the intention and smartly moved the undercarriage lever to the 'UP' position. The crew had little time for prayers but what few they managed to get in were certainly answered, for the aircraft eventually came rest with the bomb load intact and the crew uninjured! Another incident concerned one of the newer crews who, after a hectic time over the target ('All the guns seemed to be firing at *us*!') brought back a wizard photo of Leipzig. The only snag was that the target on that particular night was Potsdam! 'Finger-trouble' also affected the ground crews from time to time, as one engineer discovered whilst running-up his engines. He started all four without trouble, got convincing readings on all four rev-counters, and was then horrified to find – on looking out of the windows – that only three props were turning! And finally, there was the crazy journey of Freddy Keeler's kite when it tried to taxi round the perimeter track. After some difficulty in getting out of dispersal, Freddy spent some time on the grass before regaining the peri-track, narrowly missed clouting a Mosquito, swerved in the direction of a hangar door and had to be towed back, felt his way cautiously round to the taxiing-post and promptly ran off the road and bogged-down in the soft ground. Freddy was not amused – neither was the CO! The inquest revealed that the feed-line to one of the brakes was completely blocked.

The worst nights during my trip-free period were those on which the squadron was operating. In the traditional manner, I would watch the take-off from the end of the runway and give the old thumbs-up sign to the boys as they swung into wind, and then I would potter back to the Mess as the Lancs. circled overhead. But I rarely slept on the nights when Freddy Keeler was operating. In imagination I covered every mile of the trip and found little rest until the first distant drone of engines heralded the return of the squadron. Soon the drone would grow to a steady roar as the boys took up position in the circuit and waited for permission to land. As each aircraft made its approach, with the familiar rising engine-note as the engineer brought the pitch levers to 'fully fine', and then touched down to the medley of popping exhausts and squealing tyres, I would count off the landings. Oftimes, the returns did not tally with the number of those who had set out on the trip, and then I would start to panic. Who was missing? Probably someone had been delayed or diverted, or maybe boobed and landed at a nearby 'drome by mistake. I would picture the boys rolling in for debriefing; heavy-eyed, grubby, talking in unnaturally loud voices – a word for the ever-smiling padre as he proffered cigarettes – handing in reports to the technical types and wishing they wouldn't ask so many questions about trifles like wrecked engines or busted H2S sets – the first sip of the rum-laced tea as it found its way down a parched throat – answering the clipped, searching questions of Air Vice-Marshal Bennett, who sometimes dropped in to have a word with the crews – and trying to reconstruct the night's work for the benefit of the Intelligence Officers. Down in the Mess dining room, crews would be laughing and joking over their bacon-and-eggs, and empty beer bottles would be clattering back to their crates as some crew celebrated their screening. And then my room door would swing open and in would walk Freddy Keeler. His face would light up when he found me still awake and his smile was worth the sleepless night. It had been a 'bang-on attack' – it always was a bang-on attack according to Freddy! As he undressed, he would keep up a running conversation, giving me a rough outline of the trip and the latest gen on the missing kites; and then he would climb into his bed, slump back on the pillow and retire from the conversation.

The Air/Sea Rescue Section was coming on apace. The CO had offered to fly me over to his previous station, with a view to picking up a few tips from their section, but I tactfully talked myself out of the trip. On the day I installed the final piece of equipment, I rang the 'Wingco' and invited him to inspect a *real* Air/Sea Rescue Section. I couldn't resist a smirk of self-satisfaction at his whistle of surprise as he entered my place, for I had worked really hard to make a decent section. I took him round the exhibits and explained the construction and use of each article of equipment. He was genuinely delighted with the set-up – from the fully-equipped Lancaster dinghy with its crew of life-size dummy airmen, to the tiny CO_2 bottle of a Mae West. As he eventually left the section, he smiled and said, 'Forget about that trip, sorry I ever mentioned it'!

Over at the engineers' section there had been another welcome addition in the person of Flying Officer George Bashford, a second-tour type who soon made himself at home. The section was running very smoothly under Brooky's leadership and it seemed to me that we engineers had commanded greater respect from the rest of the squadron since he took over. This improvement in the stock of engineers was also noticeable in a wider sphere, for the flight engineer had at last worn down the suspicion – almost resentment – of the earlier Wellington and Whitley crews who, on conversion to four-engined aircraft, had looked upon the engineer almost as an interloper. Since those days, the engineer had proved himself a valuable asset and was probably the most versatile member of the crew. There were types who had taken over the 'driver's seat' in an emergency and had brought aircraft and crew safely back to base; others had manned gun-turrets to great effect, whilst on PFF the F/E had shown that he was the equal of a straight bomb-aimer.

In many ways, my second tour was proving very different from my first. Perhaps the most noticeable feature was the virtual disappearance of the 'enemy coast'. In 1943 we had to gain almost operational height over base before proceeding to battle our way into the continent, whereas in 1945 we stooged merrily across France or the Low Countries at a reasonable altitude, often over brightly-lit cities and villages. The dreaded fighter boxes and searchlight belts, which had stretched across Occupied Europe, were things of the past, and the bomb aimer's 'We are crossing the coast NOW!' had become a comment of navigational interest rather than a grim reminder that every mile flown eastward would be contested. In place of the coastline as a division, we had got the bomb-line, and that was a very different affair altogether. From day to day, and even from hour to hour, the coloured string on the map in the briefing room – indicating the line behind which bombs could not be dropped without endangering our own ground troops – moved steadily into Germany and, in doing so, robbed us of many favourite targets of the past. Another feature lay in the direction of the attack; from Elsham we rendezvoused at points on the East Coast, usually at Mablethorpe, Sheringham, Skegness or Cromer; but from Upwood it was mainly south, Selsey Bill, Beachy Head or Brighton, invariably via Reading. The daylight raids, of course, formed another outstanding difference and served to stress the depleted state of the German defences – the idea of a daylight raid on the Ruhr in 1943 would have been fantastic. Even in the offensive nature of the enemy there had been a great change, for in place of the flares and flashes of the typical blitz, which we sometimes used to see over Hull or Grimsby on our return from a trip, we had become accustomed to seeing the trails of V2 rocket bombs as they ascended from their launching-sites into the stratosphere, *en route* for the London area. And a further sign of the times was the addition to our escape kit of a celluloid wallet containing a reproduction of the Union Jack and the magic words, *Ya Anglichanen.*

These flags were issued to us on trips which took us close to the rapidly advancing Russian front line, the idea being that they should be worn across the chest by crews who had to bale out on the Russian side, in order that the trigger-happy Red Army types should not fire on their allies. The general feeling amongst crews was that, flag or no flag, they would be very careful about being rescued by the Russians; there were even those who said they would prefer to take their chance with the Germans.

I started April with a burst of three night trips in the first week and it was grand to get back on ops again. I flew to Lutzkendorf with the Australian, Derramore-Denver; to Hamburg with Peter Hague (a very pleasant run, vastly different from that meteorological shambles which was still referred to as 'THE Hamburg trip'); and to Plauen with Denver who was Deputy Master Bomber. I enjoyed flying with 'Derry', for I already knew some of his crew; the navigators, George Kay and Tiny Walters had been in the Toddy crew and the rear gunner, 'Mac' McQueen, had the rack next to mine in the locker room.

My next trip was to Schwandorf with 'Jimmy' James and this proved a very interesting affair. Jimmy was Deputy Master Bomber on the attack and, in view of the fact that we would be spending some time over the target, I was asked by Group to take a colour film of the proceedings. On the way to the target I missed a scoop when I couldn't grab the cine-camera fast enough to get a few shots of a collision between two Lancs. which caught fire and plunged to earth in flames. Over Schwandorf, Jimmy was doing orbits to starboard so that I could film from my side window but to get decent shooting angles I had to hang half-way out of the open window, without gloves, goggles or helmet, and this proved quite an experience. My eyes and ears took a beating and – trifling as this incident was by comparison – I did get some little idea of the tremendous courage needed by those heroes who had climbed out on to the wings of aircraft in attempts to put out fires.

The Allied armies were chasing the Hun all over the continent and because of this our next trip, a daylight to Bremen, was a very ticklish operation. The 'brown jobs' were reported to be on the outskirts of the port and we were supposed to do a spot of tactical bombing to ease their task. The bomb-line was shifting about like a wriggling snake and all the way to the target I had the feeling that the town would be taken before we arrived. But I was wrong, for Bremen was still spiteful and the flak was coming up thick and fast. The attack demanded perfect visibility but unfortunately clouds began to shroud the target area as we were running in, and the Master Bomber wisely decided to scrub round the bombing. In a selfish sort of way, we took rather a dim view of the army – they were pinching all our targets and besieging cities which we had always considered our own particular property!

My log-book told me that Bremen was my twenty-fourth trip with PFF and I needed only one more to complete my second tour. But the sands were running fast and it was beginning to look as though the war would end before I logged the twenty-fifth. I prayed for a speedy ending to the war but added a rider that I might just make that last trip. On the last day of April, I got my wish; I was on the battle-order with Jimmy James in 'D-Dog'. But how different was the briefing; no Master Bomber's call-sign to memorise, no intricate details of bombing priorities, no checking of bomb stations and switches, and no bombs. True, we were carrying marker flares, but for a very different purpose from that to which we were accustomed. It was the queerest briefing I had ever attended and as I walked down to the locker room with the rest of the crew, I felt that I was dreaming the whole thing. We were going to Rotterdam on 'Operation Manna' to mark an area for the dropping of food for the people of Holland. The route was straight out and back, altitude under 1,000 feet, no cameras to be carried in the aircraft, no orbiting the target, and all arranged in collaboration with the Germans, who promised that there would be no interference with the operation! No wonder the boys looked stupefied. After years of slaughter and desolation, we were going out in the guise of angels of mercy. We swished across the North Sea at 'nought feet' and on reaching the coast, climbed slightly and flew over villages and farms to our target. Every man, woman and child who could wave a welcome was out there in the streets and fields; there were tablecloths, towels, carpets, scarves, flags, everything that would flutter; I saw one laddie waving a flag as he cycled along; unfortunately he topped into a ditch, unequal to the task of gazing upwards and watching the road at the same time. But it was in the city of Rotterdam that we really saw what the RAF meant to the gallant Dutch. Every flat roof-top had its contingent of well-wishers and every vantage point – from ladders to attic windows – was manned to get as near as possible to the low-flying Lancasters. It was the maddest, merriest sight I had ever witnessed. I was very close to tears and there was no need to hide the fact; the other boys were equally affected. I could read the signs over the shops and smiled when I noticed one with 'KEOHLER' in bold letters – I hoped Freddy Keeler would see it, might be a 'Dutch uncle' of his! As we ran in to drop our flares, I saw a kite lob a marker smack into the front garden of a house. I felt annoyed about this boob but the spectators seemed to look upon the incident as part of the fun, so I presumed there were no casualties. I also noticed several squads of German troops and it must have been very galling to have such wonderful targets without being able to do anything about it. The return to base was made in almost complete silence, each man occupied with his own thoughts, each feeling that the war was virtually over.

In the week that followed the trip to Rotterdam, rumour was quickly followed by counter-rumour; the war was over, it was not over; but in the midst of all the confusion, one thing was certain enough for me, I was going on leave on the 7th of May. On the journey north, I attempted to sort out the jumbled mass of memories which crowded my mind like the pieces of a vast jig-saw puzzle. There had been so much to think about, so much to learn in the past few years that I was unable to build up a complete picture. But certain things pushed themselves to the front, determined to be noticed. There was the memory of Jack Osborne smiling at me and methodically tapping a Player's 'Medium' on his cigarette-case – of my Indian friend of St Athan days assuring me that my 'lifeline' was good – Dot beside me at the altar steps on our wedding day – Jimmy Green banging his fists on the plaster jacket which held together his fractured spine, and demanding 'Go on, hit me! I'm cast-iron!' – Bill Smith with his whimsical smile and his inevitable phrase 'Believe you me' – riggers painting 'W' on the nose of a brand-new Lancaster – my pal of Aldergrove days, 'Steve' Stevens, monopolising the jukebox at the Ritz cinema café in Belfast – Freddy Keeler dashing into our room with news of the latest battle-order, and his excited cry, 'You're on! You're on!' – the chuckles of Syd Horton as he related how he and Bob Parkinson waded into their German guards and continued their escape journey through France – and, running through all the memories, the haunting strains of Chesterton's crew-song:

> '. . . Cologne, Wuppertal, Bochum, Dusseldorf,
> They are just an awful mess.
> Berlin, Hanover, Mannheim, Hamburg,
> All aboard for the "Deutschland Express!"'!'

116

There were kisses and handshakes when I entered my home. In Britain, this was the day of joy and thankfulness. That evening the voice of Winston Churchill – the voice which had rallied Britain in her hour of despair at Dunkirk, the voice which had spurred her on to a complete and shattering victory – announced that Tuesday, the 8th of May 1945, would be remembered, for all time, as 'VE Day'.

It was all over in the West! It was all over!

CHAPTER SIX

WANDERING WINGS

There was an official code-name for the trips to newly-conquered Germany, but we called them 'loot runs'. It was only natural that after an overnight stay in Hamburg or some other city of the Third Reich, bods should return with souvenirs of their visit, but the size and value of these reached such alarming proportions that – with reports from other squadrons of ambitious types who had landed with racehorses and even small yachts on board – it became obvious that the limit had been reached and that authority would clamp down on the traffic. By the time this stage came, however, a fair amount of booty had been brought over and most bedrooms in our Mess had been stocked with interesting things. There were steel helmets, ceremonial swords, officers' full-dress uniforms, revolvers, silver swastikas, Luftwaffe pilots' log-books, aircraft instruments, watches, pens, cameras, radio sets, and suchlike useful or ornamental goods.

I did not feel too happy about the souvenir-hunting for, with the average Englishman's weakness of feeling sympathy for the beaten foe, I was working up to a sneaking admiration for various elements in the German armed forces. For the night fighter crews who mixed it to such deadly effect with our bombers; for the flak-gunners who so accurately and persistently defended their blazing towns; for the army types who held out in pockets of resistance like Brest and Dunkirk; and even for the better type of U-boat crew. But the admiration was short-lived. Authentic reports and photographs of the German concentration camps at Belsen, Buchenwald, Dachau and other places, began to trickle through and the world vomited its disgust. The slight softening in my attitude towards the Germans was wiped out in an instant by the proof that they, as a nation, had committed or condoned such wholesale, cold-blooded slaughter. It was reasonable to assume that we in Britain would have been weeded-out in similar fashion – a solemn thought to retain for a very long time and not to be lightly thrown aside.

In the excitement of VE, we seemed to have temporarily forgotten that World War II was by no means over. Grim battles were still being fought in the Far East against the other enemy, Japan. It came, therefore, as rather a shock when the Wingco gathered the squadron together for the purpose of sorting out personnel to be transferred to 'Tiger Force'. Apparently, this was to be a Bomber Command outfit for service against the Japs, and popular rumour had it that the bases used would be on certain islands in the Pacific. According to the gen, chaps who had completed two tours of ops or had an early Release Group number would not be included in the scheme; nor would the Commonwealth types, because they were already making preparations to return to their home countries. Crews not detailed for Tiger Force would probably go on Transport Command, and rumour posted them to India for trips 'over the hump'. There did not seem to be any great enthusiasm for either project and the thought of the squadron breaking up did nothing to raise the general morale.

Amidst the welter of confusion and rumour, I received a letter from home which made me realise that even though the shooting war was over, the pastime of aeronautics was still fraught with danger. The news was that Cousin Harold had been reported missing from an operation. After an operational career of many years, with Bomber and Coastal Commands, Harold had been allowed to taste the joys of victory and then, two days after VE, Fate had snatched the cup away. There was no information as to the nature of the operation on which Harold had been engaged and so I could not speculate on the possible reasons for his failure to return. I could only hope that there would soon be news of his safety.

Bomber Command was doing a number of jobs which were foreign to its nature, and the happiest of these were the trips to continental airfields for the purpose of picking up Allied ex-prisoners of war and returning them to their homeland. I flew on one of these trips with the Station Commander, Group Captain Menual, and we had as passenger the new AOC, Air Vice-Marshal Walmesley. The trip over to Juvincourt, France, was made of extra interest by the slight diversion from track during which the AVM searched for, and found, the spot where he had landed after baling out from a Halifax early in the war. He pointed excitedly to a low wall behind which he had hidden his 'chute and harness, and then he traced his journey to a nearby wood and to the village where he had subsequently taken refuge. It must have been a great thrill for him to see those places from the air. The touch-down at the 'drome was pretty grim, I thought we were never going to stop bouncing, but our landing was mild in comparison with the efforts of some of the others. The runway was in bad condition due to bombing and had the contour of a switch-back. There was every prospect of fun-and-games at take-off. We had been warned to taxi carefully on the steel-mesh perimeter track but there wasn't much chance of avoiding tyre trouble with the 'heavies' and on checking the wheels after parking the kite, I found four nasty gashes in the walls of our tyres. I decided against a wheel-change, however, and informed 'Groupy' that I considered the tyres OK for the return trip. Bearing in mind the state of the runway and the presence of our distinguished passenger, I hoped K-King would not let me down. The rest of the kites were filling up with ex-POWs and, as our crew had nothing to do until 'Groupy', who was in charge of the operation, was through for the day, we chatted with various groups of newly-released men and searched for familiar faces, though without success. Each aircraft had welcoming messages chalked around the entrance door and I saw lots of chaps writing their names and thanks on the sides of the fuse-lage as they waited to climb in. With the exception of several aircraft held back for tyre changes, the operation moved smoothly along and in the late afternoon 'Groupy' completed his duties and we returned to base.

Ever since Wingco Craig took over command of the squadron, we had a religious service once a week in the crew room. Padre Bullen led a few simple prayers and then, after the Wingco had read a lesson from the Bible, we sang a couple of popular hymns to the accompani-ment of Flight Lieutenant Yendell's accordion. The service was a splendid innovation and was much appreciated by the boys. It was, then, with very sincere regret that we crowded into the crew room one morning, to say farewell to Padre Bullen, who was taking his release from the RAF. In making the presentation of a silver cigarette-case, the CO expressed all our sentiments when he said that the padre had been the best-loved man on the station and that the boys of 156 Squadron would never forget his constant attendance at debriefing, where his welcoming smile and cheery words had meant so much to returning crews. The padre, in reply, thanked us for the gift and said that he had tried his best to bring true happiness to the squadron. He recalled the names of many of those who had never returned and his voice trembled with sincerity when he declared that his part was a very minor one compared with that of the lads who had given their lives or freedom in the cause of peace.

To counterbalance the loss of Padre Bullen and a few of the older stalwarts on the non-flying side of the squadron, we had the great joy of welcoming back three lads who had been prisoners-of-war. The first of these was the rear gunner of Evans' crew and he was given a tremendous reception. On the night of the fateful trip, he had been searching the sky for enemy fighters when a series of violent shudders had shaken the aircraft and sent her plunging down out of control. The skipper, Evans, had given a 'Prepare to abandon aircraft!' order as he had fought the stick and, after acknowledging the warning, the rear gunner had tried to release his turret doors but found that they had jammed. He had been on the point of advising the skipper about this when the aircraft had resumed its normal attitude and the order had been countermanded. But this good news was barely acknowledged when a terrific explosion had taken place. When the gunner had regained consciousness he was lying on grass, with his opened 'chute straining at his harness straps. For a man trapped in a turret with jammed doors, this was a near-miracle and he had immediately taken advantage of the fact. Determined to get through to the Allied lines, then nearing Germany, he had walked for twelve days and most of twelve nights; but with success almost within grasp, he had been captured. Captured because he had torn the soles of his feet to ribbons after wearing out first his flying boots and then his socks! Captured because he had been forced – in sheer desperation – to take a rest on a wayside seat and had then found it physically impossible to stand up again! After having been battered into unconsciousness by a gang of German youths, he had been taken over by the military police and then handed into the care of the *Luftwaffe*. Transferred to hospital, he had received every attention from the doctors. New soles had been grafted on to his mangled feet and in the many weeks of the treatment, the scars left by the mauling he had received at the hands of the Hitler Youth had been gradually erased from his face. As the Allies advanced, he had been moved deeper into Germany but had been released eventually when his camp had been over-run.

Our next re-union was with Flying Officer Evans, who was able to fill in some of the gaps in the gunner's story and also relate his own adventures. At the moment of the explosion which had knocked the rear gunner unconscious, Evans had been normally seated with hands gripping the wheel of the control column, feet in the straps of the rudder bar and body held firm to his seat by the Sutton harness. He, also, must have lost consciousness for on opening his eyes he had found himself in mid-air, still holding the control column and with the Sutton harness straps still round his body. In a dazed sort of way, he had glanced down and seen the Lanc. breaking up into several parts. In the open end of the centre section of the fuselage, stood a figure which had hesitated for a second or so and then launched itself into space, to be blotted out almost immediately by the opening of a parachute. The sight of the white canopy had prompted Evans to think of his own safety and, after discarding the control column, he had pulled his rip-cord and in due course arrived on German soil. His attempt at escape had been short-lived, for he had soon been picked up by Jerry and deposited in a prisoner-of-war camp. He had later made contact with his wireless operator, who had said that he had just risen from his seat to unclip his parachute-pack when the kite had blown up and a heaven-sent parachute-exit had appeared at his feet, so he had tumbled out and pulled the string. We were bitterly disappointed to learn that there was no news of the engineer, Freddy Parr, or the rest of the crew.

The night of Flying Officer Pelly's return to the squadron was the occasion of a double-barrelled celebration. Not only was he toasted as an ex-POW but also as a potential bridegroom, for he was to be married on the following day. Jack Cornelius was to be best man and he came along to the party. It was good to see that Corny had discarded his crutches, although the wounded leg was still giving trouble and causing him to hobble. We had a whale of a night and although I didn't manage to get the full story of Pelly's Cologne trip, I learned that he had made a successful bale-out but was later captured by the Germans. I did not find out what had happened to the rest of the crew.

It must have been in deference to the excellent organisation of the firm which specialised in conducted, Continental travel that the series of post-war flights over Germany were known as 'Cook's Tours'. The general idea was that the boys who had been accustomed to bombing targets from altitudes of 20,000 feet or more – usually at night – should have the opportunity of examining the results of their efforts under more favourable conditions. By taking along the ground-staff bods as passengers, the aircrews were also able to show their appreciation of the grand work done by the lads who 'kept 'em flying' throughout those difficult years. It was possible, too, for the intelligence, met., flying control, medical and other non-flying sections to be given a glimpse of the places which had concerned them in one way or another but had been just names on a map. In addition, it was a pleasant way of spending a summer afternoon.

Two routes were chosen for the tours; Route 'A' embraced towns in the Ruhr Valley and points east as far as Hanover; whilst Route 'B' took in towns along the Rhine as far as Mannheim. The trips were a terrific success and there was much competition and a certain amount of flannelling to get on the 'battle-order'. As a free-lance, I did not find it easy to wangle into a crew detailed for the north-west route, but I finally managed a trip with Flight Lieutenant George Beca in P-Peter. The ground crew lads we were taking along were quite excited at the prospect of flying over Germany, though not more excited than we at the thought of returning – like murderers of fiction – to the scenes of our crimes.

On the outward route, we crossed Walcheren Island and from our operational height of 1,000 feet were able to see clearly the breach made in the sea-wall at Westkapelle – a fine bit of bombing which caused widespread flooding, much to the discomfiture of the enemy troops which were gunning the ships making for Antwerp. The first sight of a German town was for our passengers a grim introduction to the things which were to follow. Wesel was the point at which the 21st Army Group crossed the Rhine, after a softening-up by the RAF which did nothing to improve the appearance of the town. The effect on the ground-crew lads was staggering. Their experiences of the blitzes on British cities, and particularly their own personal bomb-story, faded into insignifance in the light of what Bomber Command had done to Germany. Wesel, they noticed, was not blitzed – it was pulverised. Riding down the Rhine through Hamborn to Duisburg, whose extensive docks had been somewhat disarranged by countless cookies and incendiaries, we turned into the 'Happy Valley' of treasured memory. Fast as the ruined cities slipped beneath our wings, thoughts of exciting nights over the Ruhr came crowding back to me. My eyes feasted on the twisted agony of Essen, but inwardly I saw the red and green target indicators dripping down on to the target, like Bessemer-converters spewing exotically-coloured, molten metal; saw the flame-torn, smoke-belching eruption which was a town undergoing a saturation raid. And at Gelsenkirchen the synthetic oil plants were a shambles, but through the mangled pipelines I saw again that blazing Halifax which had uncannily followed 'W-for-William' for miles before blowing up, and I wondered if pieces of that unfortunate aircraft still lay amongst the wreckage below. Bochum – Dortmund – Kamen – Soest – each name conjured up some vision of the days that were gone, and each carried its own memory of lads who had never returned from attacks on those towns. Leaving behind the Ruhr Valley, we set course for Bielefeld – where Bomber Command had breached an important viaduct, a fine example of precision bombing – and so through Herford and Hildesheim to our turning point at Hanover. Dear old Hanover! Along with Cologne, it was my most-visited target, for on four occasions had I heard the cry of 'Bombs going!' whilst stooging over its unhappy streets. Westward then to Osnabrück and the self-satisfying sight of its battered buildings. We left Germany by way of Münster, Emmerich and Cleve, and flew over Nijmegen and Arnhem, where wrecked gliders and fabric-strewn trees marked the ground which would for ever be sacred to the memory of the airborne troops who had so gloriously failed to hold a too-powerful enemy at bay.

Crossing the coast at The Hague, we set course for base and arrived back after a six hours trip which had been full of interest. As I entered the flying time in my log-book, I wondered idly if 'Butch' Harris had organised himself a super-Cook's Tour; it seemed appropriate that the 'Hammer of the Reich' should survey the results of the repeated blows he had struck on the land of the crooked cross.

On the day following my trip round Germany, I received grand news of Cousin Harold. He was safe and well. Beyond the fact that he had been involved in a ditching, there were no details of his escapade but the important thing was that he was OK.

The good news was quickly followed by word from the Adjutant, Flight Lieutenant 'Taffy' Williams, that I had got the Permanent Award of the Pathfinder Badge. I positively glowed with pride – I was a Pathfinder for all time!

But the day was not without its sorrow. My very good friend Freddy Keeler was informed by the Adj. that he had been posted to Transport Command for training, prior to service with that outfit in the Middle East. It was a blow for both of us. Three days later, Freddy Keeler packed his bags and was on his way. The things I had intended to say, somehow remained unsaid, and it was only in the firmness of my handshake that I could try to convey to Freddy just what his friendship had meant to me and how much I would miss him.

*   *   *

124

During my tour as in instructor at Seighford, I had made an intensive study of everything connected with Air/Sea Rescue and had attempted to further those studies by applying for a course of instruction at the School of Air/Sea Rescue, Blackpool, but was informed that the Station ASR Officer had already taken the course and thus it was unnecessary for me to do so. I was very disappointed. It was, then, with great delight that I learned from Wingo Craig that he had arranged for me to take the course which had, in the meantime, been transferred to the flying boat base at Calshot.

The course provided an instructive and enjoyable fortnight, during which I took part in Air/Sea Rescue searches, sailed in high-speed launches, dinghies of all types, airborne lifeboats, and inspected the new long-range boats – powered by four Packard-Merlins and controlled by a flight engineer. The instructors at the school put the various subjects over in an interesting manner and I left Calshot with a host of happy memories and the conviction that the course had been well worth while.

On my return to Upwood, I found the squadron in a state of turmoil. Leave had been cancelled and there was a great deal of re-shuffling amongst the crews. I gathered that Tiger Force had been modified – or postponed, or scrubbed, no one seemed to know just what was happening – and that '156' was moving over to Wyton. The gen on the movement was that complete crews were staying with the squadron and that all spare bods were being posted. I took a very dim view, not only because I had expected to get leave at the end of the ASR course but also because I was still a free-lance and was faced with the alarming prospect of leaving the squadron. But there was no need to panic, for good friends had been pulling strings during my absence. I learned, with relief, that I had been officially crewed-up with Flying Officer Lemon and that I would be OK for leave as soon as we had settled down at the new station.

By a smart bit of organisation, Brooky and Bash wangled themselves into the advance party which was going over to make the billeting arrangements, and with two such expert foragers at work on our behalf, it was a foregone conclusion that we engineers would fare well in the allocation of rooms. On the morning of the move, the boys of '156' paraded for the last time at Upwood, and then piled into crew-coaches or private cars. We were given a great send-off by the people staying behind at Upwood and also by the local villagers who turned up in strength to wave farewell. The crews who had been detailed to fly the aircraft over, paid their respects by shooting-up the 'drome and the village in the time-honoured manner. Rad and I drove over in his car and on arrival we contacted Brooky, who assured us that everything was fixed. The squadron had taken over the west wing of the Mess and the old firm of Ash, Bash, Brooky and Rad, was established in adjoining rooms. I was sharing a room with Flight Lieutenant Jenkinson, a second-tour pilot who had recently joined the squadron, and as far as I was concerned the arrangement was quite satisfactory; 'Jenks' being a fellow-Lancastrian and a good type to boot. We had the services of a civilian batman, who soon gave evidence of his ability to deliver a tactful and well-brewed early-morning cup of tea.

In general layout, Wyton was very similar to Upwood; both stations were peacetime efforts, with main buildings and hangars identical in appearance though not in position. Wyton, however, had a distinguishing feature in the huge, concrete water-tower which dominated the view from almost every angle; with a cylindrical body and streamlined supporting fins, it looked like an outsize V2 rocket in firing position. Office accommodation for the squadron was much the same as that provided at Upwood and the various sections soon settled down to the old routine. As the station already had a fairly good ASR Section, I had little trouble in licking it into shape, and was able to concentrate on arranging for leave, negotiations for which were successfully concluded on my third day at Wyton.

Leaving Rad in charge of the section, Brooky, Bash and I piled into the Jaguar and headed north for Sheffield; I with the prospect of seven days' leave, and my companions with thoughts of a crafty weekend lengthened by virtue of our overnight start. On arrival at Sheffield, Brooky ran us round to his home – where his wife sportingly made us an early-morning meal – and then, after a pleasant chat over cigarettes, to the station where Bash and I boarded a Lancashire-bound train. When I arrived home, Dot and the folks were still abed but insisted on rising to prepare breakfast. For the second time in a few hours, I sat down to bacon-and-eggs.

Breakfast over, we discussed matters of general interest and then I learned that Jack Osborne's mother had received word that Jack was buried in a Dutch cemetery. This sad news was later followed by a letter from a Dutch family who were tending Jack's grave; they also enclosed a photograph of the grave, on which could be seen a white cross bearing Jack's service number, rank and name.

It was fortunate that I had arrived home early, for I was able to see

Cousin Harold before he returned from leave. He was apparently none the worse for his ditching and was inclined to be flippant about the whole thing. Beyond accepting my congratulations with good grace and advising me to 'get some ditching hours in', he contented himself with gloating over the little goldfish emblem pinned to his tunic. I realised that it was going to be difficult to get his story out of him, but I had the bright idea of approaching the subject from a purely technical angle, stressing that his experiences would be of value to me when lecturing on Air/Sea Rescue. The tactics worked like a charm and, aided by gentle prodding from time to time, the whole story was prised loose.

Two days after VE, Harold and crew had taken off from Great Dunmow in Stirling 'S-Sugar', carrying a payload of eighteen paratroops and their equipment as part of Operation 'Gaerdamöen' which had been laid on as part of the plan to occupy Norway at the end of hostilities. The met. forecast from Norway had promised good flying conditions but this had proved far from the truth and 'Sugar' had soon been in difficulties. Sleet, snow and icing conditions generally, had beset the aircraft and after wandering blindly around for what had seemed hours, they had eventually been forced to ditch on a lake in Sweden. Unfortunately, the lake had proved to be partially covered with timber logs and the Stirling had broken its back at the moment of impact. Four paratroopers had been killed and three others had sustained injuries. After a brief sojourn in Sweden, the survivors had made their way to Oslo and had eventually been ferried back to base. The story was told with a wealth of detail which reflected great credit on the crew and passengers, and on the Swedish troops who later took them in hand.

I was sitting in the section, chatting to the boys, when the CO rang through and asked me to go up to his room. 'This,' thought I, 'is it!' My posting, without a doubt! The Wingco greeted me with a smile, waved in the direction of a chair and proffered a cigarette. I pulled up the indicated chair, selected a cigarette and settled down to hear the good news – my reception had ruled out any question of posting. The Wingco informed me that I had been chosen to be a member of a crew which would shortly be proceeding on an important mission to a foreign country. The whole thing was to be a frightfully 'priv' effort, a trip for which every aircrew type in the RAF would willingly give his right arm. I made the appropriate, appreciative noises and pumped the CO for further information but, beyond the fact that I was relieved of all squadron and station duties for the ensuing six or seven weeks, there was nothing to learn.

After lunch, the CO called me again and I entered the room to find five of the squadron stalwarts already installed; I drew up a chair and the Wingco proceeded to give us the dope. We six would form the crew for the special mission and would have about a fortnight in which to make our preparations. We were to spend as much time together as possible, both on duty (flying) and on social occasions, and we were to treat the CO's room as our crew room. A squadron aircraft was to be prepared for the trip and certain members of the ground staff would be chosen to act as servicing personnel. I glanced at the men who were to be my companions. The pilot was Squadron Leader Ken Letford, DSO, DFC, 'A' Flight Commander; the navigators, Squadron Leaders Freddy Chandler, DSO, DFC, and 'Blackie' Blackadder, DFC, Navigation Leader; the wireless operator was Flight Lieutenant Tommy Greene, DFC, Signals Leader; and the rear gunner, Flight Lieutenant Johnny Cooper, DFC, the Gunnery Leader. The six of us had completed a total of 444 operational trips during the war – a gen crew by any standards.

On the following day, the 'priv' crew went to London for yellow-fever injections and a spot of shopping. Instructions had been given that our uniforms had to be in perfect condition and that we were expected to have civilian clothing, so there was a regular stampede to Simpson's and Austin Reed's to replace battered hats and suchlike articles which had seen more than a little service. We lunched at the Wings Club and, after another session round the shops, grabbed a hasty tea before claiming our seats at the Ambassadors, where we saw Hermione Gingold at her wittiest in *Sweeter and Lower*. After the show, we met Jacko – rear gunner in the old Toddy crew – who took us to a favourite spot of his for a late meal. We spent the night in town and continued our shopping in the morning and then, fortified by a splendid lunch at Simpson's, returned to camp with our purchases and depleted clothing books. Being a crafty, thrifty type, I wangled a week-end pass so that I could bring my pre-war clothing from home. The folks were very surprised and pleased to see me and were soon asking me about the forthcoming trip but I was unable to enlighten them – for the simple reason that I hadn't got a clue, and wouldn't have been able to say anything if I had.

There was a surprise waiting for me when I returned to Wyton. The Wingco called a conference and informed us that the mission had been extended in scope. Three special aircraft were to be prepared for the trip, two being crewed by other squadrons and the third by '156' as already arranged. There were, however, two alterations in our crew, the Wingco himself would be taking over in place of Ken Letford and, as it had been decided to dispense with the rear gunner, Johnny Cooper was out. This was a bitter blow for Ken and Johnny, and we all felt very sorry about the whole business. Further gen on the aircraft was that they would be brand-new Lancaster VIIs – a Mark which combined features of the Lancaster and the new Lincoln – and were expected to be ready for air-testing before the end of the week. The squadron was seething with curiosity and when they saw us carrying tropical kit from the Main Stores, the wiseheads murmured 'Middle East!' whilst more ambitious prophets asserted 'Pacific!'

I had just returned from a visit to the camp tailor's when Brooky told me that there was a telegram for me. I took the slip of paper from the rack and read the message, 'CONGRATULATIONS ON AWARD OF D.F.C. LOVE. DOT.' My heart gave a violent thump and my mouth felt suddenly and strangely dry. The DFC! The news was so wonderful that I hardly dared believe it. But on the following day, I learned from the Adj. that the award was officially through and the confirmation was hotly followed by a spate of letters and telegrams from relatives and friends, who had seen announcements in local and provincial newspapers. Then my father rang through to offer his congratulations. I was walking in the clouds! And then my thoughts went back once more to the days at St Athan when Jack and I had assured each other that honour and distinction would be ours in the fullness of time. But the sands had run too swift for Jack. If only he could have been with me to share my joy, and that he too could have realised his ambition. That evening, the Mess Tannoy invited 'all members of 156 Squadron to join Flying Officer Ashton, DFC, at the bar'.

At our next conference the Wingco gave us full details of the mission. Our VIP passengers were to be Air Chief Marshal Sir Arthur Harris, Colonel Hecksher (Air Attaché to the Brazilian Embassy), and a highly-influential Brazilian with his young daughter. Our destination was Brazil. It was to be a mission of the greatest importance and, as we were to be the guests of the Brazilian Government, hospitality would be on the very highest level. It followed, therefore, that we were expected to comport ourselves as ambassadors of the Royal Air

A brand new Lancaster VII being prepared for the special mission to Brazil

Force and of Britain. There was one other item of news which gave great pleasure to our boys, a member of one of the other crews had withdrawn from the mission and Johnny Cooper had been selected to take his place.

130

Our personal preparations were almost complete and we were asked to take our kit along to the crewroom for inspection by the Senior Air Staff Officer, Air Commodore Boyce. The purpose of this was to ensure that each man carried a suitable wardrobe and to check our passports and chits for injections and vaccinations.

Our three aircraft, 'Abel', 'Baker' and 'Charlie' – resplendent in a finish of white with glossy black undersides – had been taken up on air tests to get the snags ironed out and our final trip was a consumption test. We stooged across France to Marseilles, altered course over the Gulf of Lyons, and ran north of the Pyrenees until we reached the Bay of Biscay, just south of Bordeaux, where we swung north for Brest and Cornwall; the run back to base being made via the Isle of Man. We maintained an indicated airspeed of 150 knots, at 8,000 feet, and our fuel consumption for the airborne time of over ten hours was 178 gallons per hour – an excellent figure. 'Baker' had no major snags and the crew worked together in a delightful manner. My mascot 'Joe' was already at his post, hard by the helmeted-head of the Wingco. With such a crew, and such an aircraft, I looked forward to the mission with an eagerness matched only by my impatience to meet again the man who was respected and idolised by every aircrew type who had flown under his command – 'Bomber' Harris.

CHAPTER SEVEN

SPECIAL MISSION

It may have been that expected absence was already making the heart grow fonder, but the English countryside had never looked lovelier than it did during our leisurely stooge down to the rendezvous point at St Mawgan. So glorious was the morning that we were almost sorry to reach the Cornish 'drome, but once down on the deck, we felt the excitement of the forthcoming trip and forgot our premature pangs of homesickness. The third Lanc., 'A-Abel', had already arrived, so we repaired to the Mess where we contacted her skipper, Wing Commander 'Jock' Calder, and the rest of the crew. Squadron Leader 'Jock' Cairns, in 'C-Charlie', had accompanied us on the trip down, so the aircrew party was now complete and, as St Mawgan was standing treat, we were all able to make friends and discuss mutual interests in an atmosphere of cordiality and anticipation. As we were staying the night at St Mawgan, our crew decided to pay a visit to neighbouring Newquay and after a pleasant day we retired early to bed.

On the following day – Tuesday, the 24th of July 1945 – the BBC announced that Air Chief Marshal Sir Arthur Harris, accompanied by personnel of Bomber Command flying Lancaster aircraft, was proceeding on a Special Mission to Brazil. This announcement was also carried by the daily press, so we knew that the long-suffering types at Wyton would have been put out of their misery.

At briefing, we had just been informed that our diversion on the first leg of the trip was the runway at Gibraltar, when the briefing officer glanced towards the door and gave us the signal to rise. We were shuffling awkwardly to our feet when the Air Chief Marshal entered the room and I felt a terrific thrill at the sight of our great leader. The ACM immediately set the tone for the whole trip by a nonchalant wave of the hand and the request, 'Sit down, please – no fuss!' The remark took my mind back to the day at Elsham Wolds when he had joined battle with the boys of 103 Squadron on the

132

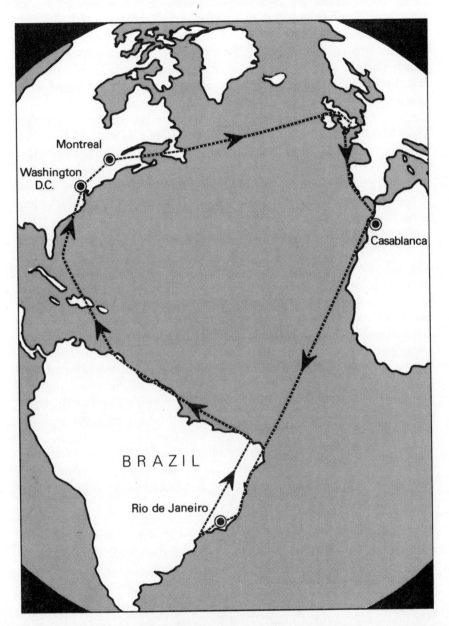

Route taken during the 'Special Mission' to Brazil

subject of bomber equipment and tactics. I remembered that the gunners had made some very candid remarks about the 'point-three-o-three' Brownings fitted to their Frazer-Nash turrets and had pleaded for the more potent 'point-five' guns. It seemed rather ironic that the turrets fitted for the forthcoming trip were equipped with 'point-fives' – the first I had ever seen in Lanc. turrets.

At the conclusion of the briefing, we were introduced to the Air Chief Marshal and his party, which consisted of his Personal Assistant (flying with the ACM in Jock Calder's 'A-Abel'); Colonel Hecksher, the Brazilian Air Attaché (with Jock Cairns in 'C-Charlie'); and the Brazilian and his daughter (with Alan Craig in 'B-Baker'). The atmosphere was delightfully informal and we all felt that the trip was going to be fabulous.

Out at dispersal, I made an exhaustive check of 'Baker' and, after ground-testing the engines, set about the business of preparing for take-off. The night was pitch dark, relieved only by the aircraft interior lights and navigation lights, and the waving beams of the torches wielded by our starting-up gang. As the crew climbed on board with their equipment, I made conversation with the little girl, in an attempt to ease what must have been for one of her tender years, a somewhat awe-inspiring experience – for a night take-off was not the pleasantest of thrills even for a grown-up. Completely unruffled, Miss Seven-years-old confided that she had often flown before, including Atlantic crossings in 'Clipper' aircraft! I picked up the tiny, specially-designed harness and parachute, and escorted the veteran flier to her seat.

'Abel' was first off the deck and then, at precisely fifty-three minutes to midnight, 'Baker' took the air, closely followed by 'Charlie'. The long days of preparation, secrecy and anticipation were over – the Special Mission to Brazil had started.

The briefing officer at St Mawgan had been at pains to warn us against flying over neutral Portugal and we registered conscientious surprise when we saw the lights of Lisbon below. No doubt an adverse wind had blown us slightly off track, but it was convenient that it should have done so at that particular position for the sight of the illuminated city made a pleasant change from the darkness. The rest of the trip was somewhat monotonous, as 'Baker' was in grand form and we welcomed the spot of bother with the intercom. system, which led to amusing communications written on scraps of paper.

The first stage of our trip was completed when we lobbed down at

Rabat Salé, in French Morocco, after a flying time of exactly seven hours. RAF servicing personnel swarmed over the aircraft almost as soon as the props stopped turning and it looked as though our stay was to be short and sweet. I outlined a few snags to 'Chiefy' Loach (who was in charge of the ground crew we were taking with us to service the aircraft) and then, using the cockpit as a dressing-room, did a quick change into tropical kit, for even at that early hour the temperature was uncomfortably high. The 'drome was very modern in appearance, having permanent hangars and other buildings; with runways, perimeter tracks and roads of concrete; and living quarters and messes of the usual pre-cast type. There were several Dakotas and Liberators sprinkled about the place and, apart from the heat and the sand, one might have been on any sizeable aerodrome in Britain. That illusion was dispelled at breakfast by the presence of Moroccan waiters and by the lashings of bacon-and-egg and the liberal supply of fresh fruit. Jock Calder and crew made a late appearance at the Mess and it was evident from their faces that something was amiss. The engineer, Alan Palmer, told me that the servicing gang had found a considerable quantity of engine-oil in 'Abel's' port-inner coolant tank and that the system was being drained and flushed. It later transpired that subsequent running tests had proved unsatisfactory, with the result that a signal had been sent to the UK for a new Merlin engine to be flown out to Rabat. Orders were given to transfer the ACM's luggage and pennant to 'Baker'. The mission was to press-on and the disappointed crew of 'Abel' were to follow when the new

A-Abel – in distinctive white and black finish – undergoing an engine change at Rabat, North Africa

motor had been installed. We sympathised with Calder and his boys but our sympathy was turned to chagrin when we learned that a further decision to reshuffle the crews and passengers had been made, and we of Craig's crew had the disconsolation of watching the other kites take off whilst we kicked our heels on the deck. Beyond wiring 'Joe' into the new aircraft and stowing away our luggage, there was nothing we could do to help on 'Abel', so we eagerly accepted the Station Commander's offer to take us into the city of Rabat. Our party, now consisting of Colonel Hecksher and the crew, climbed into the big Humber staff-car and were whisked at high speed along the very fine roads into the city.

After surveying the city from the flat-topped roof of an hotel, we decided to take a closer look at the more-accessible showpieces and headed first for the Cathedral. This twin-towered building was very beautiful inside, with some superb mosaics depicting the Stations of the Cross. After taking a few photographs, we walked along the tree-fringed road to the Medina, where the Moors conducted their business from tiny, open-fronted shops flanking the narrow streets. Trade was brisk and was conducted in a babel of threats and argument, the best bargain apparently being struck by the one who could shout the loudest. I was intrigued by one character who was making cycle-tyres from old car inner-tubes – an ingenious yet simple method whereby the inner-tubes were cut into discs about the size of a penny and then threaded on to a length of wire until there were sufficient to encircle a cycle wheel, the ends of the wire were then fastened together and the result was a serviceable, puncture-proof tyre. We next visited the Sultan's Palace, where we were shown the robes and regalia worn by Sultans of bygone days, together with many valuables and trinkets of precious stones and metals. Outdoors, in the terraced gardens, we examined what must have been the prototype of all water-wheels – a wooden contraption which lifted water from a well by means of earthenware pitchers, deposited it into troughs and thence by easy stages to all parts of the fine gardens. Motive power was provided by a donkey, harnessed to an outrigger from the vertical shaft, which was crudely 'bevelled' into the water wheel – the output was not impressive! Before returning to camp, we did a round of the night spots and this gave me the opportunity to discuss Brazil with Colonel Hecksher. The Colonel was very proud of his country and assured me that we were going to have a wonderful time. He raved about Rio and insisted that it was the most beautiful city on earth. Brazil was going to be one of the most important – if not *the* most important – countries in the world when she really got down to the business of developing her vast natural resources. His conversation fascinated me, and the others who had joined in, but much as we would have liked to continue until the early hours, we decided to return to camp for some sleep – our first for two days.

On the following morning we were informed that there was little likelihood of 'Abel' being serviceable before midnight, so we 'borrowed' the Station Commander and his car once again and paid another visit to the city. Down at the hotel, we found the British types in a state of considerable excitement, for the General Election results had just come through and showed that the Socialists had been returned with a big majority. The news was staggering – perhaps not so much from the purely political angle, but because it seemed that Winston Churchill had been cast aside in the very hour of his triumph. We stayed in Rabat until tea-time and then returned to see how the engine-change was progressing.

Shortly before midnight, I got the OK for ground-testing and after a run-up and final check-over, I decided that everything was bang-on. With almost two days' leeway to make up on the other kites, we had to press-on pretty rapidly and at 2.15 a.m. the Wingco eased 'Abel' off the runway at Rabat Salé and we shook the sand of Morocco from our wheels.

It was rather a pity that the flight to Bathurst was made at night, as we had looked forward to seeing some of the interesting places along our route. We should have seen the Atlas Mountains far away on the port beam and, with a dog-leg to starboard, could have seen the Canary Islands – particularly Tenerife. And then there was Casablanca itself. How demoralising it would be to admit that one had been to Morocco and had not seen Casablanca, even from the air! However, we did appreciate the coolness of the night and had reached Dakar before we began to feel the heat of the morning sun. At 1040 hours we sighted Yumdum Airfield, near the mouth of the River Gambia, and lobbed down a few minutes later. Whilst the rest of the crew and the passengers made for the control tower, I stayed behind to superintend the refuelling – our next leg was a night crossing of the South Atlantic and I wanted to make sure that the tanks were definitely full. On leaving the aircraft, I was hailed by a hearty type who insisted on running me down to the Mess on the pillion-seat of his motor-cycle. After a refreshing shower I sat in the Ante Room to await the arrival of the crew, but in vain. Frantic telephoning finally elicited the information that the party was being entertained at the British Airways Mess at Fajara – I was at the RAF Mess at Yumdum! Transport was organised and I was driven down to Fajara by one of the native 'boys', who did things with a wheeled vehicle that I would not have believed possible. To my surprise, we arrived at our destination in one piece and I was more than thankful to tumble into bed for a spot of sleep.

It was almost dark when I was turfed out of bed to join the rest of the lads in a cooling shower before walking over to dinner, and the darkness owed as much to the threatening clouds as to the approach of nightfall. In the Mess, we chatted with several Ferry Command types and I noticed that they always referred to Britain as UK, a term that had also been used by the chaps at Rabat. It would have been nice to have spent a full day at Bathurst but we were still a long way behind 'Baker' and 'Charlie', so we dragged ourselves out of the comfortable chairs and piled into the cars which ran us back to Yumdum. On the way over, the weather took a definite turn for the worse and, by the time we had reached 'Abel', had developed into a full-blooded tropical storm. At twenty minutes past midnight, we turned the aircraft on to the runway and with not a few fervent prayers, opened up the engines. The blackness of the night and the fury of the storm brought visibility down to a few yards and the runway lights were hardly discernible. We belted into the unknown at peak revs for what seemed hours and then ever so gently the Wingco nursed back the stick and 'Abel' slid gratefully off the deck. It was one of the finest and 'gutsiest' take-offs I had ever seen – and certainly one of the most thrilling. We did a circuit over the now-invisible drome and set course for the Atlantic Ocean, the Equator and South America.

There should have been something dramatic about flying the Atlantic for the first time but the crew and passengers of 'Abel' couldn't have cared less. The passengers slept most of the way and the crew plugged along with the old familiar routine of going places in the dark. Even the fact that we were 'crossing the line' passed almost without comment. The Wingco had changed over to my seat and he was soon asleep – having not the slightest interest in degrees of latitude or longitude. Piloting a heavy bomber at night – at least, on a peaceful night – was probably one of the most tiring and tedious of occupations and when I took over the driver's seat, I dosed myself with 'wakee-wakee' tablets and took a generous swig of coffee. No matter how hard one tried to concentrate or how limply one relaxed, the luminous needles and figures of the instruments seemed to have an hypnotic effect. In my own seat I could always twiddle adjustments, finger check switches and levers, or work on my log, but in the pilot's seat there was nothing to do but just sit and watch the panel. With the automatic pilot engaged, it was even worse, for drowsiness was then accompanied by a nagging whisper to 'Leave it to "George", take a quick nod, you'll be OK'!

With the coming of dawn, however, the boredom of the night vanished and we began to feel the excitement stealing up on us with every mile flown towards the land of promise. The sun – which was now in the north – turned on its heat and the cockpit soon became unbearably hot. I detached several fibreboard panels from the sides of the fuselage and fixed them round the canopy but even with an almost complete blackout, we still had to doff our shirts to keep cool. There was never at any time any suspicion that our motors might falter or develop undue thirst and we eventually droned over the north-east shoulder of Brazil, dead on track and dead on time, without having wasted a second thought on the airstrip at Ascension Island which was to have been our diversion point in the event of trouble. Exactly nine hours fifteen minutes after leaving Africa, we touched down on the wide, concrete runway at Recife Airport; just in time to exchange greetings with the crews of 'Baker' and 'Charlie' who were preparing for the final stages of the journey.

Any prospects of sleep we might have entertained, were shattered by the news that we had to catch up the other kites before they reached Rio, and we had very little time in which to have a shower, change from tropical kit into battledress, and stow away a hearty breakfast. Refuelling was completed by the time we returned to 'Abel' and with a minimum of fuss, we bade *Au revoir* to our hosts at Recife and nipped smartly into the air.

Our Atlantic crossing had been carried out at an indicated airspeed of 155 knots but as we hustled south down the coast of Brazil we whipped the speed up to 200 knots and made our rendezvous point – several miles north of Rio – almost bang on time. The other Lancs, however, were nowhere in sight and had evidently decided to press on, so we continued in solitary splendour.

There are, in the lives of most people, occasions which justify the remark, 'I shall remember this moment until the day I die'! Such an occasion was our introduction to Rio. We had descended from 10,000 feet at our rendezvous point to a more respectable altitude and were fussing around doing the checking and tidying-up which usually preceded a landing, when an excited shout from the Colonel – who was down in the bomb aimer's compartment – brought everyone rushing forward to the cockpit windows. Visibility was not too good, due to the heat haze, but we could just make out the shape of a bay in the far distance. For the minute, there was nothing spectacular to see and then, as though a curtain had been drawn aside, we were rewarded by the most beautiful sight in all the world. To the south and to the east, as far as the eye could see, stretched the green expanse of the Atlantic Ocean; from a fantastic bay, islands rose like the coils of a prehistoric sea-monster; and on the golden sands of many beaches, white-capped rollers broke with gay abandon in great clouds of spray. Conspicuous in shape and perched precariously on the edge of the land-mass, was a small mountain which even I – whose only knowledge of Brazil was limited to the recollections of a cinema 'Travelogue' – recognised immediately as the world-famous Sugar Loaf. Spreading inland from the sea to the slopes of tree-clad mountains, standing sentinel-like against the cloud-flecked sky, was a boulevard-edged fairyland, glittering in the golden sunshine with all the fascination of a tray of diamonds. There, in that setting of Technicolour run riot, lay the exotic city of Rio de Janeiro. Freddy Chandler was the first to break the silence, with a remark that summed up the feelings of all, 'I don't believe it! I just don't believe it'!

We did a couple of circuits in salute and then settled down to the landing. According to original instructions, the mission was scheduled to lob down at a 'drome many miles outside Rio, for the simple reason that the runway at the city's Santos Dumont Airport was too short for four-engined aircraft – it was an 'impossible' 'drome for the heavies. The largest kite to land there was that three-engined slow-coach, the Junkers 52; attempts had been made at various times to bring in Flying Fortresses but these were unsuccessful. The ACM decided that the Lancs *would* land at Santos Dumont. As the Wingco took 'Abel' over the runway to size up the situation, I wondered if 'Butch' had not been just a wee bit rash, for the airport was built out into the bay, with a single, short runway starting and ending in the sea – it would be like landing on a stationary aircraft carrier. But there on the deck, surrounded by milling crowds of sightseers, stood 'Baker' and 'Charlie', so the job was obviously possible. Losing height gradually and with full flap coming on, the Wingco made a grand approach and as we wafted over the near edge of the runway, I cut the throttles and 'Abel' sank to the deck with a screech as the tyres scrubbed the concrete. In a remarkably short distance, thirty tons of

The author checks the gauges during the approach to Santos Dumont Airport

Lancaster was brought down to walking pace and turned smartly on to the grass to take up position with the other aircraft. By dint of hard flying on our part, with very little sleep for the past five days, the mission to Brazil was complete once more, and after making running-down checks, we descended the steps of the ladder to greet our hosts.

During those very few minutes between retiring to bed and falling to sleep on my first night at the Hotel Gloria, I reviewed the events of a very exciting day. The Atlantic crossing, the run down the coast, the glory of Rio from the air, and then the reception at the airport. We were honoured by the presence of His Excellency the Ambassador, the Naval, Military and Air Attachés, the Consul, and many other representatives of Britain; Brazilian civil authorities were there in strength, and the Brazilian Air Force was represented by high-ranking officers and a Guard of Honour. Press photographers, reporters, newsreel cameramen and radio commentators fluttered around like a lot of excited hens. After introductions, salutes and handshakes, we made our way to the fleet of cars which had been placed at our disposal and, escorted by speed-cops mounted on siren-shrieking motor cycles, made a triumphant entry into Rio de Janeiro.

It had not been possible to arrange accommodation in one hotel, so it was decided to split the party into three sections, with the officers at the Copacabana Palace Hotel and the Hotel Gloria, and the ground-crew NCOs at the Hotel Pax. The party was also split up for the purpose of allocating English-speaking, Brazilian Air Force officers, whose duty it was to act as interpreters and chaperones, and generally smooth our way during the visit. We were a party of five at the Gloria – Alan, Freddy, Bill, Lofty and myself – and we were attended by *Capitáo Aviador* Umberto Luz de Aguiar; a handsome, smartly-uniformed officer who hastened to assure us that he was 'Umberto' to his friends. Over a splendid meal, served in our suite, Umberto gave us a rough outline of the programme arranged for the fourteen days we were to spend in Rio, and he promised that we would be given a wonderful time. It was whilst looking at the booklet produced for the visit, that we discovered that Freddy spoke excellent Spanish and was able to read the booklet – printed in Portuguese – with very little trouble. Freddy was going to be a useful man to have around. The cover of the booklet carried the colours of the Royal Air Force and the *Fôrça Aérea Brasileira* (FAB), and I was surprised to learn therefrom that in Brazil, 'Brazil' was spelled '*Brasil*'. By the time we had reached the coffee stage, we had learned many things about the United States of Brazil, not the least interesting of which was the fact that her size was greater than that of the other United States in North America, and her population less than that of the British Isles. Umberto proved to be the perfect host and his English was practically flawless; indeed, the position was such that our Service slang departed so much from the mother tongue, that it might have been thought that we were the foreigners rather than Umberto. Our jovial friend found great delight in learning to speak of 'kites' and 'prangs', and chuckled over 'a piece of cake', 'having a bash', 'putting up a black' and similar RAF phrases; whilst we, in turn, tried our tongues on *não compreendo* and *obrigado*, and wrestled with the conversion of pounds, shillings and pence into cruzeiros.

The night was yet young when Umberto said that he had reserved tables at a floor-show and the news was received with enthusiasm by the boys. On learning that it was customary for Rio to make merry until the not-so-early hours of the morning, I decided, somewhat reluctantly, to catch up on some sleep. My apologies were received with good grace by Umberto and by the boys who, unlike the crew of the lame duck 'Abel', had not missed their sleep on the trip over. On departure of the pleasure-seekers, I took a leisurely shower and then stood for a while on the balcony outside our rooms, gazing at the scintillating beauty of Rio by night. Cooled by the sweet-scented, winter breeze, I left the balcony and retired for the night – half-afraid that the waking morrow would prove that everything was just a dream.

Pyjama-clad and fresh from the showers, we breakfasted in our rooms to the accompaniment of a running conversation about the activities of the previous night. Umberto arrived in time to share coffee and cigarettes and, after greeting us individually in Latin-American fashion, he gave us an outline of the arrangements made for our first engagement. This was an informal visit to the English colony at Niteroi, across the bay from Rio. Outside the hotel, our cars were waiting to take us to the ferryboat, and we were amused to see the drivers whiling away the time by flicking dust off the coachwork with feather-dusters. O for an English winter that would warrant the use of feather-dusters!

After a pleasant sail across to Niteroi, we met the members of the Yacht Club, with whom we took cocktails before enjoying a swim from their private beach, and then went on to the Cricket Club, where lunch was served on the pavilion balcony. During the meal, we learned of the 'Bellows Club', an organisation which had raised many thousands of pounds in aid of the war effort – principally in helping to purchase Spitfires. In the afternoon, a cricket match was laid on between the ladies of the club and our boys, who were handicapped by having to bowl and bat left-handed and when the last wicket had fallen, players and spectators repaired to the pavilion for welcome drinks. Much as we would have liked to prolong our visit to lovely Niteroi, our presence was required elsewhere, so we bade our hosts *Au revoir*.

The cocktail party in the Air Attaché's apartments was a very pleasant affair which afforded the opportunity of meeting members of the British Embassy staff. Apparently, our arrival in Rio had created a terrific sensation and we had made front page news in all the daily papers. The landing at Santos Dumont came in for particular mention and the visit of the Air Chief Marshal was obviously considered by Brazil to be an occasion for general rejoicing and a very great honour. Our photographs were given great prominence and one unfortunate type had already been dubbed 'the blue-eyed baby of the party'. The Embassy staff informed us that a book of press-cuttings would be compiled for each member of the mission, thus relieving us of the trouble of wading through the papers. At the pre-arranged hour, the party broke up and we masculine types returned to our hotels for shaves, showers and a general sprucing-up, for the night was yet young and we were due to dine and dance at the Casino Copacabana.

After the austerity of war-bound Britain, dinner at the Copacabana had all the trappings of a Bacchanalian feast, and we luxury-starved visitors worked our way through the courses with a zest that surprised our hosts. The floor-show was wizard and we conceded an early point to Umberto who had asserted that the night-life of Rio was unrivalled by that of any other city in the world. We had arrived at an opportune time, for Rio was being swept by the tempestuous Samba and the rhythm of the dance, carried along by the bewildering tune 'Tico, Tico', soon had our party in its grip. That Samba had all the fervour of a ritual dance and I felt that it would always linger in my memory to remind me of Rio – just as the tune 'Maybe' instantly brought back memories of the crowded ante room at Elsham. It was at a very late hour that we eventually escorted our ladies to their homes, and three-in-the-morning before we dismissed our cars at the steps of the Gloria.

Umberto found us still abed when he called later in the morning, and he took great delight in dragging the bedclothes from our reluctant bodies. First in one room and then in the other, he chivvied his charges into bathrooms and phoned for breakfast to be served immediately; maintaining the while, good-natured leg-pulling about our particular partners of the previous evening. Fortified by food and drink, we were out to the cars in good time and joined the party from the Copacabana as they were forming up for the drive through the city. The long line of Packards, Cadillacs, Chryslers and Buicks, headed by the traffic-clearing speed-cops on their Harley-Davidsons, rolled slowly through the crowded streets, then streaked out of Rio and made for the hills. We left the well-surfaced main roads and our drivers treated us to some hectic moments on the narrow, twisting roads which led to Casa das Pedras, Tijuca, where we were to attend a Barbecue given in our honour by *Senhor* Droult Ernanny. I had often read of barbecues but had only a hazy idea of what the word meant, so it was with natural curiosity and eagerness that I joined the hundred or so guests, who were conversing in groups under the trees. The magnificence of the gardens and the size of the private swimming-pool in the valley below, suggested that this was to be a meal in the grand manner; and when I investigated the source of a fragrance which set the nostrils quivering in anticipation, I confirmed that view. Several long trenches held slow-burning fires and over these on long, sword-like skewers arranged in an inverted V, were huge steaks, fowls, lambs and other flesh of unidentified origin, all roasting to a crisp golden-brown. Hard by the fires were the carving-blocks, on which the cooks were already engaged in cutting sizzling steaks into more respectable portions. I took my place at one of the tables which were set outdoors and found them already loaded with enough food to feed a squadron of hungry airmen, and the assortment of wine-glasses at each place lent assurance that the matter of thirst had not been overlooked. We dined to the music of a *gaucho* orchestra and after doing full justice to the good things set before me, I felt that I had amply satisfied both my appetite and my curiosity.

Back in Rio, the junior types made for their hotels, whilst the ACM accompanied the Ambassador to make calls on the President of the Republic and his Ministers of State. We rejoined our chief later at a reception and cocktail party given by His Excellency at the British Embassy, and then descended in force on the Casino Urca, where a special floor-show was laid on in honour of Sir Arthur. The ACM dined with the Brazilian Air Minister and his party, and their table was the focus-point for all eyes. Time and again, 'Butch' rose to acknowledge the enthusiastic reception and we aircrew types noted that our chief seemed to be thoroughly enjoying himself. Our tables, in turn, came in for a share of the limelight and there were so many flash-bulbs pooping off that I was reminded of the flak-barrages of less-joyful occasions over Germany. Merrymaking continued far into the morning and it was not until 3.30 a.m. that we finally retired to our hotels for a very welcome sleep.

On the last day of July, our third in Rio, we travelled in convoy to the *Escola de Aeronáutica*, at *Campo dos Afonsos* (Air Training School for officer-cadets of the FAB) where our arrival was honoured by a Company of Guards. Our first visit was to the Station Commander's headquarters, where we were introduced to the officers of the school. From the outset, I was greatly impressed by all that I saw, and felt that neither expense nor trouble had been spared to give the cadets everything of the best. The airfield itself was set in beautiful surroundings and, with the inevitable blue skies for a playground, flying training must have been one, long holiday. Returning to the school

145

buildings, we inspected the troops' quarters and then visited the various sections whilst the trainees were undergoing instruction.

Having seen all the instructional side could offer, we gathered on a balcony overlooking the parade ground for a Colour Hoisting Parade of all cadets and officers stationed at the school. This was a most impressive ceremony, especially when the British and Brazilian flags were hoisted side by side, as a symbol of the great friendship of the two nations and allies. The parade – headed by a band, some ninety strong – then marched from the 'square' and passed in review, in honour of the ACM. The parade over, we joined the cadets for lunch and, to their delight, instead of confining ourselves to the usual 'top table', we split up and dined amongst them. The visit concluded with a display of 'skip-bombing' by low-flying Boston aircraft.

Following our return from the school, we went along to the Navy Club, where an informal supper/dance had been laid on so that we could meet the crew of a small ship of the Royal Navy, which had docked at Rio. The 'matelots' were a grand set of lads and we spent a jolly evening together. Our friends the Niteroi crowd (as we had christened them) were there in strength, as were our ground staff lads. Chatting with Chiefy Loach and Mac, I gathered that all the NCOs were thoroughly enjoying their stay in Rio; their time was more or less their own and apart from periodical work on the aircraft, they were able to concentrate on having a good holiday.

Early the following morning, the ACM flew to Pôrto Alegre with the Minister of Aeronautics, for the passing-out ceremony of air cadets and a review of the school, and to attend a banquet offered by the *Interventor* of the State of Rio Grande de Sul. With the boss away, we seized the opportunity to 'let our hair down' and arranged a very promising programme for the day. Our Brazilian chaperones had laid aside their uniforms and 'chicken guts' and appeared in civilian clothing, whilst we RAF types changed from best blue to more informal battledress. After breakfast, we drove to the airport where our aircraft were open to the public for inspection. On leaving the cars, we were at once besieged by autograph-hunters, headed by what seemed to be the entire female population of Rio; we autographed handbags, compacts, handkerchiefs, bank notes, dresses, bare arms and shoulders, and even autograph-books. Umberto had warned us that we were the current heart throbs but we had not reckoned on such a welcome from the charming *senhoritas*; it was, of course, good fun and we secretly adored the hero worship. Our British friends were well in evidence amongst the long queues which formed outside the entrance door of each kite and we were happy to show them what a Lanc. was like inside. For the ladies, the scrambling over the main spars proved somewhat embarrassing and to be faced with the descent of a very long ladder from the bomb-aimer's compartment to earth, proved rather more than they could bear. British and Brazilian maids alike were reluctant to display their more intimate garments to the public gaze, so we had to resort to two-way traffic through the fuselage, thereby upholding modesty but seriously impeding the morning's work. Freddy Shepherd aired his knowledge of the language amongst our Portuguese-speaking customers, whilst we coped with those who could speak English.

Some of the lads were going for an afternoon's cruise on a private luxury yacht but our party from the Gloria plumped for a spot of bathing at the fabulous Copacabana Beach. For a change, we drove leisurely through the streets and soon found that life was just as dicey as travelling at the normal flat-out speed. I had never seen cars driven along main roads like they were driven in Rio and it was a complete mystery to me why the city was not littered with wrecked cars and corpses. Everyone drove flat out and on the few occasions when a stop had to be made, this was effected by stamping the brake-pedal through the floorboards. By a series of miracles, we avoided ramming or being rammed and arrived at the Lido, shaken but intact. For ten *cruzeiros* (about 25p) we had private rooms in which to change and take a shower, the loan of swimming trunks and towels, and receipts for our valuables, which were sealed in packages and stowed away in a safe. Up to the moment when we crossed to the beach and spread our towels under one of the gay umbrellas which dotted the sands, we travellers had imagined that we had acquired a glorious sun-tan, but on seeing the bronzed figures of the Brazilians and the holiday-making Americanos and comparing them with our own Persil-white bodies, we felt like rushing from the beach in disgust. Inspired by the exuberant Umberto, the lads raced to the water's edge and proceeded to throw each other about, but I lingered a while to take stock of the world-famous beach. Copacabana! What a lilt there was in the very name and how smoothly it rolled off the tongue; mere repetition of the word was a thrill in itself. Nor did the place belie the name, for the view from my vantage point on the towel-of-many-colours must surely have been without rival. The hundred islands of the bay, the green seas breaking boisterously on the shore in a rainbow-hued mist, the voluptuous curve of the beach itself, backed by the mosaic prom-enade of the Avenida Atlantica and the glittering façade of luxury hotels and restaurants, were each beautiful in themselves but combined, and drenched with the most glorious sunshine, they left one breathless with wonder and hopelessly short of adjectives to describe the scene. However, the view was probably just as good from the water, so I joined the lads and was promptly flung into the first breaker for my tardiness. The bathing was exhilarating and we would have stayed in the water all afternoon but Umberto kept a watchful eye on the Lifeguard's tower and when the warning flag fluttered from its mast, he ushered us back to our umbrella. It seemed that although the difference between high tide and low tide was almost negligible, there were certain periods of the day when the surf and undertow became dangerous and bathing was prohibited. One thing surprised me – the sands were almost deserted.

The evening was launched at a cocktail party given by the British colony at the Paysandu Club, and from there we went on to the Casino Atlantico for dinner and dancing. During an appropriate lull in the proceedings, Umberto introduced several FAB types to our party and we were delighted to learn that they were fighter boys who had just arrived in town, after a tour of ops in the Italian theatre of war. These lads had been flying Thunderbolts and Mustangs, and we were soon swapping reminiscences. The Atlantico, however, was not the place for solid conversation and there were our ladies to consider, so we returned to our tables after making preliminary arrangements for an RAF/FAB stag party before the end of our visit. It was well after midnight when we returned to our hotels and even at that time of the day, Rio was bursting with life. A million lights made a mockery of the clock and the city became a synthetic fairyland, with a beauty almost approaching that of the daylight hours. The waters of the bays mirrored the curving necklaces of lights around the boulevards and night-eyes blinked from the skyscrapers, as though dazzled by the brilliance of the neon signs. And, barely visible in the outer ring of darkness, the fantastic silhouettes of mountains and islands. But in all that beauty, one thing stood out above everything else. On the peak of their highest mountain in Rio, the Brazilians had raised a magnificent statue of Christ and this was floodlit in such a manner that the figure dominated the sky and the city, with arms outstretched as though to bless and embrace all mankind. Of all my Rio memories, I would treasure most that of the *Corcovado* by night.

To the great relief of the car drivers, who had been on call almost continuously since our arrival at Rio, it was decided to use aircraft for the visit to São Paulo. The ACM was flying direct from Pôrto Alegre, whilst we took off from Santos Dumont in three FAB aircraft; five of us with Umberto in his twin-engined Beechcraft and the rest in two Lockheed Lodestars. As ever, the weather was glorious and we were agreeably surprised by the mountainous nature of the terrain. Someone asked Umberto what sort of a place São Paulo was and we learned that it was the biggest manufacturing city in the southern hemisphere, with a population – still growing rapidly – of about one-and-a-quarter millions. On arrival at Cumbica Airfield, we were met by a fleet of cars which whisked us to the Hotel Esplanada.

The visit to São Paulo started with a luncheon at the hotel, given in honour of the ACM by the Commander of the 4th Air Zone, *Brigadeiro* Antônio Appel Neto. Once again, I was amazed at the capacity of the human stomach and I wondered how we were going to exist on the rationed plain fare when we returned home. But that was just a fleeting thought and forgotten long before we attended our next function, a reception at the Country Club, where we met members of the British Colony.

After tea, Colonel Hecksher took me to see two cinemas, the Ipanima and the Maraba, which had recently been opened in the city.

Air Chief Marshal Sir Arthur Harris (4th from right) and Colonel Hecksher (far right) during a visit to the Brazilian air force training school

149

The managers of both these magnificent buildings were delighted to show us round and I was suitably impressed by the luxurious seating accommodation, the air conditioning and the elevators which conveyed patrons to the balconies. Smoking was banned and this helped to keep the atmosphere delightfully fresh.

Dinner at the Jequiti Bal was a very enjoyable affair and was made the occasion for a special night by the management. The tables were decorated with alternately-arranged British and Brazilian flags, in silk, and these were soon appropriated as souvenirs and passed round for autographing. Music for dancing was specially chosen and our boys went to town on the Lambeth Walk, the Chestnut Tree, the Hokey-Kokey, and other old favourites. Jock Cairns surprised the patrons – and us – by taking over several instruments in the band, and a fine job he made of it, too. During the evening, we learned that two Bostons had crashed over the city and this, naturally, cast a gloom over the gaiety of our FAB friends.

We were all sorry to hear that the ACM was indisposed and would not be able to take part in the trip to Santos. He insisted, however, that the programme should be carried out as arranged, and deputed Jock Calder to represent him. Our day started with a visit to the *Laminação Nacional de Metais*, a gigantic metal works in São Paulo, where we were conducted round the various shops by the manager and his staff. It was very interesting but I found the temperatures rather overwhelming and was glad when we wandered out-of-doors to inspect some light aircraft which had been built at the works. These were lovely little jobs and we had a busman's holiday, climbing into the cockpits and waggling the controls.

The run down to Santos provided one of the finest drives I had ever had; the roads were magnificent and the scenery beautiful. We halted for coffee at a roadside café and from there the road tumbled down the mountainside in a tortuous succession of acute hairpin bends. Stretches of the road were carried on huge viaducts, which clung to the almost vertical rock-face by sheer will-power and the grace of God, and we expected the cars to crawl down in low gear, with the brakes applied. Unfortunately for our peace of mind, the drivers decided to make a race of it and we arrived in Santos in a state of considerable agitation; though this was carefully hidden in order not to 'lose face'.

Santos, a coastal town about two hundred miles south of Rio, was a fashionable seaside resort and also a naval base, with a population of about 190,000; roughly the size of Plymouth. We motored along the promenade and, although we had no time to stop and admire the view, we did notice the lovely beach, with its background of mountains on the other side of the bay, the palm-dotted gardens dividing the road from the beach, and the mosaic sidewalks which lent an added touch of colour to an already colourful scene. Our destination was the Hotel Parque Balneário, for a banquet offered by the Interventor Federal, at which senior Naval officers were present, in addition to civic dignitaries. Everything was on the grand scale, with hundreds of roses decorating the tables, acres of silver gleaming in the light from the huge candelabra, and a battery of wine-glasses at each man's place. Courses came and went in orderly succession, the piles of cutlery dwindled and the different wines worked their way along the glasses until we were able to sit back for the speeches. Afterwards, the whole party retired to the balcony for the benefit of Press photographers and newsreel cameramen, and then we bade our hosts 'Good-bye' and pressed on to the next engagement. This was a reception at the Santos Athletic Club, where we met members of the British colony. We would have liked to stay on for the Ball which had been arranged for the evening but, unfortunately, our time was limited as we had to be back in São Paulo before nightfall. In any case, we didn't relish the idea of negotiating the mountain road in the dark.

The *Brigadeiro*'s Cadillac set a cracking pace on the run back to São Paulo and we screamed up the mountain pass like competitors in an Alpine speed-trial. Having gained the summit, the drivers slammed their accelerators down to the boards and we swept along in line astern at speeds in the region of ninety miles per hour. It was too much to expect that we could get away with race-track driving on the public highway for very long and it was hardly surprising that we were involved in an incident which might have had serious results. We were driving flat out when our driver pulled out to overtake a coach, leaving himself just enough room to miss another coach travelling in the opposite direction; unfortunately, another car pulled out from behind the second coach, right in our path, and a head-on crash seemed inevitable. Our driver – without a moment's hesitation, and without lifting his foot – swung the car back on to its own side of the road, deliberately hitting the side of the coach in order to gain the necessary road space. A glance back through the rear window showed that we had ripped the front mudwing off the coach, but our man just pressed on. A few miles outside São Paulo, the Cadillac began to ease up and eventually stopped, whereupon the whole convoy pulled to the side of the road. Apparently, the high-speed run had boiled the water in the Cad's cooling system, for clouds of steam issued forth when the driver lifted the bonnet to investigate. Rather foolishly – I thought – he started to unscrew the header-tank cap, with the result that a jet of scalding steam and water shot out as the cap came off. That, in itself, would have been of little consequence, had not the *Brigadeiro* been standing close by in an inquisitive attitude. As always happens in these cases, the *Brigadeiro* was at the receiving end of the jet, and the ensuing flow of Portuguese had to be heard to be believed. After allowing the car and the *Brigadeiro* time to cool down, we restarted and toured slowly into the city; our driver chastened by the damage to the door panels and mudguards of his own car, which he had examined during the stop.

We dined that night at the Roof Club and, once again, sambas and rumbas were interspersed by British tunes and dances. The night-club had a bar which was decorated in an unusual manner, the walls being covered with the front pages of newspapers from all over the world. These had been pasted on higgledy-piggledy and then varnished over, the effect was really good and very interesting. This was our last night in São Paulo and, although we had been away only two days, it seemed ages since we left Santos Dumont airport.

Our stay in Rio was short, for we had barely time to collect fresh clothing before our convoy formed up again and headed once more for the mountains, but this time in a northerly direction. The stream of American cars had a stranger in its midst, in the form of the Ambassador's Rolls-Royce and it was a pleasure to see that most dignified of all cars streaking along the winding roads. Our im-mediate destination was Petropolis, for the lunch offered by *Senhor* Franklin Sampaio at his country residence, but we halted *en route* for cocktails at another of *Senhor* Sampaio's residences. This was a magnificent building, with a fine art gallery and library, but the most interesting feature was the Moorish courtyard, round which the house was built. As we drifted out to the cars, after our short stay, Lofty Rodwell and I were chatting with the Ambassador, and His Excellency invited us to accompany him in the Rolls, so that we could continue the conversation. The run to Petropolis was very pleasant and after leaving that town we turned into a lovely valley, where the road was definitely second-class. Our destination was a large building in the hunting-lodge tradition, with animal-skin rugs on the floors and a variety of stuffed heads and guns on the walls of the rooms. Lunch was served outdoors under a huge pergola-like structure, over which rose trees climbed in hundreds, and music was provided by two orchestras. After lunch, we wandered through the beautiful gardens and inspected the private zoo which contained some fine animals. The ACM, who had recovered from his temporary indisposition, was showing great interest in the mountain lions and we kept our fingers crossed in case our host insisted on presenting him with one of the more vicious specimens. Happily, the position did not arise, for the afternoon was slipping by and we had to take our leave for the final stage of our journey.

There are some things in this world about which there is no argument. Thus, when mountains are mentioned, one may state without the slightest fear of contradiction, that Everest is the highest; if ships are the subject of discussion, no one will deny that the 'Queens' are the biggest and most luxurious vessels afloat; and there are no challengers to the whale in the animal heavyweight class. Into that category of things beyond compare, must surely go the Hotel Quitandinha. This amazing place is situated in the mountains north of Rio, about 7,000 feet above sea-level. It is almost a town in itself – containing a shopping arcade, night club, casino, cinema, ballroom, indoor swimming pool, in addition to the usual amenities of a luxury-hotel; and having in its grounds a horse-riding academy, golf course, lakes for boating, lakeside cafés, outdoor swimming pools, tennis courts, and sports grounds to cater for every taste. The Brazilians claimed that the Quitandinha was the finest hotel in the world – the rooms allotted to our party were being used for the very first time, proof enough that it was also the most modern. The hotel was *en fête* in honour of the ACM and after the usual prodigious dinner, we repaired to the night-club, where a special floor-show had been arranged. Once again, there was an enthusiastic reception for Sir Arthur and when he had acknowledged the cheers of the crowd by a few words over the microphone, the party was on and we settled down for another wizard session.

It must have been three o'clock in the morning when Freddy Shepherd and I drifted along to the rooms we were sharing, and even at that early hour I was impressed enough by my surroundings to make a tour of inspection. We had an entrance hall with cloakroom and baggage room; bathroom fitted with bath, shower, washbowl, foot-bath and toilet; twin-bedded room with dressing tables, wardrobes, bookcases, bedside tables, chairs, divans, telephones and radio; a writing room with desks and chairs; and a french-windowed sun balcony. But it was not so much the size of the rooms or the furnishings which captured the attention, it was the superb quality of everything, down to the smallest detail. And the private rooms were a mere drop in an ocean of beauty and quality. I could imagine the Brazilian Government saying, 'Here is a blank cheque with unlimited backing, scour the world for the finest craftsmen and the finest materials, choose the perfect site, take all the time you need, and build an hotel that will be without equal – build the Quitandinha!'

After breakfast, we spent the morning pottering round the grounds of the hotel, lunched at the Lakeside Room and then sunned ourselves on the verandah whilst we made plans for the afternoon. We had all received invitations to attend the *Grande Premio Brasil* at the famous Jockey Club racecourse in Rio, but as several of us had promised to attend a cocktail party at the Paysandu Club, the party split up so that we could be represented at both events. After a very pleasant time at the Paysandu, I went on to a private dinner party and then back to bed at the Gloria, in preparation for another crowded day of life in Rio.

There was a great crowd of sightseers and the usual coterie of Press photographers, newsreel cameramen and radio commentators at Santos Dumont airport – as befitted an occasion when the President and his honoured guests were to pay homage to the memory of a national hero. The RAF and the FAB were to lay wreaths on the monument built to the memory of a man who was one of the pioneers of flying in heavier-than-air machines, Alberto Santos Dumont. Many Brazilians claim that he achieved flight before the Wright brothers but, although that claim may be disputed, there is no doubt that Santos Dumont was one of the great aeronauts. It is said that Dumont died of a broken heart; that when Federal aircraft bombed the rebels of São Paulo into submission during the revolution of 1932, he became so dispirited at the uses to which the machine he had helped to pioneer was being put, that he felt life was no longer worth living. So great was the reputation of the man, that when news of his death became known, messages of sympathy were dropped on the city by aircraft which had previously dropped bombs. For the ceremony at the airport named after him, airmen of the two nations stood side-by-side, *cáqui* and blue uniforms alternating, and saluted the memory of one who had tried to benefit mankind.

During the afternoon, we went to Copacabana Beach for a swim and a laze in the sun, and there we learned a rather interesting thing about the sand. Having already agreed that it was the cleanest, driest, finest and best-coloured we had ever seen, there seemed little else one could say about sand; but Rio had to be just that little bit different by also having musical sand! When Umberto remarked on the fact, we were inclined to scoff, but on stamping a foot or thrusting a fist into the sand, we were rewarded by a distinct, musical note. Whilst discussing the reason for this phenomenon, we heard something which made us look instinctively at the sky; it was the roar of aero-engines more potent than those which wuffled their way over Rio. Although none of us had ever seen a Superfort in the flesh before, we instantly recognised the slim, purposeful lines of the latest American bomber, which was operating so successfully in the Far East. The Superfort presented a lovely sight as it flew over the city and we guessed that she must be carrying General Ira Eaker, who was due to arrive in Rio that day. The point that interested us was whether an attempt would be made to land at Santos Dumont, but when we saw the aircraft heading inland we knew that our feat of bringing in four-engined bombers was not to be challenged.

There was an innovation in the arrangements for dinner, in that we reverted to our crew state and dined at different places. We, of Craig's crew, helped to make up a party of twelve at the Naval Attaché's suite and we spent a very enjoyable evening. After dinner, the parties converged on the Ambassador's residence for the Ball given by His Excellency. On arrival, we were presented and then made our way to the ballroom, where we found many old friends and were intro-duced to many new ones. The Ball was a brilliant affair and thoroughly enjoyable, though tinged by the knowledge that it was the last big function of our visit. Festivities continued far into the night and, even when our cars began to arrive, there was an invitation from the commander of the Naval craft to go out to his ship and carry on the party until the crack of dawn. For those with the prospect of a lazy day ahead, it was a grand opportunity for a full session and some of the boys went along, but we Gloria types were flying in the morning, so we decided to excuse ourselves.

Umberto was very concerned to find that Bill was not feeling too good next morning and advised calling in a doctor, but Bill insisted that he would be OK, though not equal to joining us on the sched-uled trip to *Citade dos Motores*. Almost certainly, the trouble was caused by the abundance of rich food which his stomach had found too much of a good thing after years of plain fare. So, leaving the invalid to the tender care of the room waiter, we hurried down to the airport where Umberto's Beechcraft was already being warmed-up. Half-an-hour or so later, we lobbed down at a small grass 'drome from which we travelled by estate-car to the *Fábrica Nacional de Motores*, the aero-engine factory we were to inspect. There, we met *Senhor* Edmund M. Carli, who greeted us in perfect English and, after a pleasant chat in his office – when we learned that he had been educated at Oxford – we started on a tour of the works. Everything about the place was new and there were several departments which were still unfinished. The general idea seemed to be that the production under licence of medium-powered Pratt & Whitney radial engines had been started, with a view to 'running-in' the works and training the employees. I was particularly impressed by the engine-testing department, where engines could be given running tests under conditions approaching those experienced in flight, the engines being controlled and checked from soundproof control-rooms, divided from the 'din-house' by glass walls. It was interesting to note that the entire works was air-conditioned and that fluorescent lighting had been installed throughout. The welfare of employees was obviously being given every consideration, for labour-saving devices were incorporated wherever possible and the layout of the plant was such that each employee had room to move around without bumping into anything or anyone. A five-day week of forty hours was in operation and it seemed to me that a very happy spirit prevailed throughout the works.

Outside the factory, we saw vast areas of land being cleared for the construction of more factories and for a town to house the workers. I commented on the presence of several large hills in the district and *Senhor* Carli replied that they would be moved when the land was needed for building. And that was not intended as a joke, as I first thought, for soon afterwards we saw a hill actually in process of being moved. Batteries of extra high-pressure water jets were trained on the hill which, ever so slowly but surely, was being washed away; water and eroded material being conveyed by canals to low-lying areas.

We took lunch in the very fine clubhouse and here again there was much to see; including an interesting museum, well-kept 'lawns' which never needed cutting – being carpets of dwarf plants which looked exactly like grass lawns, except for the colour which was rather a deep shade of green – and the woodwork of the various rooms and furniture. The wood was more than something to be admired, it was an education! Some types looked just like marble and were as hard as marble, whilst others had the most beautiful grains. I thought that there was perhaps some truth in the claim that the Amazon region contained over twenty-thousand different kinds of wood. We were more than sorry when the time came to say farewell and were all agreed that the morning had been profitably spent.

Back in Rio, we fulfilled a long-standing engagement to accompany our good friends, the Niteroi crowd, on a shopping expedition. The scene, as we sauntered along the *Avenida Rio Branco*, was both colourful and exciting. The tree-fringed road, the mosaic sidewalks, the gay dresses of the women and the oftimes gayer clothes of the men, combined with the lavish displays in shop windows, presented a picture of luxury and plenty. In some of the side-streets, I was intrigued by a fragrant breeze, which I found was due to the intermittent spraying of scent from openings above the doorways of the drug stores.

On returning to the hotel with our purchases, we found that Bill had recovered somewhat but was not yet equal to facing Rio's night-life, so I arranged to 'organise' two of the Niteroi girls to make up a party of four for dinner at the Gloria.

We had promised to display our kites to the officer cadets at *Campo dos Afonsos* and there was quite a thrill in taking up the Lancs. after their enforced idleness and a satisfaction in returning to our own aircraft, 'B-Baker'. We announced our arrival at the School by sweeping across the 'drome in close formation at nought feet. The cadets gave us an enthusiastic welcome and we spent a very happy time showing them over the aircraft and answering some of their questions. Unfortunately, our stay was very short for we had to continue our journey to Santa Cruz. The ACM had decided that a full-load take-off from Santos Dumont was not practicable and so we were to fly over to Santa Cruz, leave the aircraft there to be prepared for the return trip home, and ferry our luggage over in FAB aircraft at the end of our stay in Rio. Bad boy 'Abel' developed engine trouble once more after the take-off from Campo dos Afonsos, and Jock Calder feathered the motor and returned to Rio so that the ground crew could fix the snags and get the kite serviceable before 'Baker' and 'Charlie' left for home. As we joined the circuit at Santa Cruz, a Superfort flew alongside and we delayed our landing to have fun with our American counterpart. We found that the Yanks had bags of speed but when the Wingco put 'Baker' into a few extra-tight turns, they decided to give us best and broke off for their landing. I had wondered why the name 'Santa Cruz' had a familiar ring and, on sighting an immense hangar, remembered that the place had been the port-of-call – or the terminus – for the famous *Graf Zeppelin* on her pre-war flights to South America, and the hangar must have been used to house the German giant.

We returned once more to Rio, where we Gloria types had an invitation to dine at the flat of one of our friends. It was great fun – there were so many people there that a running buffet was organised and we sat wherever there was an untenanted space, including the floor! From there we went on to the Air Attaché's apartments for a farewell supper-party, where the fun continued until the early hours of the morning. We had the autochange radiogram to provide music for dancing and we insisted on having 'Tico, Tico' in every batch. But amidst the gaiety, the general conversation amongst the menfolk was on a more serious note than at any time since our trip started. We were reminded that a war still raged in the Far East and that during our almost complete isolation from world news, events had been taking place which might have far-reaching consequences. The Americans had announced that an 'atomic' bomb had been dropped on a place called Hiroshima, in Japan. Knowing the Yanks' love of exaggeration, some of us were inclined to scoff at this latest piece of ballyhoo and assured ourselves that the RAF still possessed the world's most potent bomb, in the 'Ten-Ton Tessie'. Another item of news was that Russia had declared war on Japan. No one seemed wildly enthusiastic about our Ally's belated decision but all agreed that anything which helped to bring the war to a speedy and victorious conclusion was a good thing; differences could then be thrashed out round the conference table and plans made for a brave, new world. And on that note of hope, we finally took leave of our hosts, not caring to remind ourselves that for many of our friends, our 'Good-night' was also 'Good-bye'.

On our last full day in Rio, the chief topic of conversation was the return trip. We had understood that our route would be the reverse of the outward journey but the jungle-telegraph now reported that the ACM had decided to take his boys on a real tour. The most popular rumour was that the return would be made via Bermuda and the Azores, although the more ambitious West Indies – USA – Iceland rumour also had its adherents. 'Abel' was still unserviceable and was to wait for a new engine which was being flown down from Canada. The new crew arrangements were that Jock Cairns would be staying behind in Rio, Jock Calder was flying 'Baker', whilst Alan Craig would take over 'C-Charlie'. Chiefy Loach would be in charge of the engine-change and would return with Cairns.

As we had no social engagements, the day was spent quietly; most people did a spot of shopping in the morning and in the afternoon we sunned ourselves on the beach, and then returned to our hotels to pack. Freddy, Bill and I dined with the British Consul, Mr Clinton, at the Gloria and were able to express our thanks for the assistance he had given during our stay. To finish off the evening, we took the cars round the city for a last glimpse of Rio by night. Our drivers seemed quite affected by our impending departure and we, in turn, were sorry to be leaving them. They had been really wonderful and had worked like slaves, with never a complaint at the shocking hours we kept.

Santos Dumont airport was crowded with well-wishers as we prepared to depart and, after our luggage had been stowed away in Lieutenant Wandersley's Lodestar, we stood around in groups, chatting with our own particular friends. There were so many people to thank for our wonderful time in Rio de Janeiro and so little time left in which to thank them, that it was impossible to get round to everybody. But to British and Brazilians alike, we felt we owed a debt of gratitude which could never be repaid; though they insisted that their hospitality was just a token of their appreciation of the work of the RAF in general and Bomber Command in particular.

And what could we Gloria boys say to Umberto? We had grown to love him as a brother, and now that we had to say 'Good-bye' we were unable to tell him what a grand companion he had been. Instead of praise, we had wisecracks, and his kindly embrace for each of us, brought only teasing remarks about his waist-line. But however flippant our words, we knew that we would never forget *Capitão Aviador* Umberto Luz de Aguiar – 'Umberto' to his friends! As the Lodestar taxied round the perimeter track to the end of the runway, we crowded to the windows for a final wave of farewell and then settled into our seats for the short trip over to Santa Cruz.

'B-Baker' and 'C-Charlie' had already been serviced when we arrived, so we had the luggage winched up into the bomb-bays, made pre-flight checks, took on board our passengers: Sir Arthur; his PA; Colonel Hecksher; and the ground staff lads who were not staying behind for the engine-change, and started on the first stage of our long journey home.

After an uneventful trip of almost seven hours, we lobbed down at Natal, on the north-eastern shoulder of Brazil, and were promptly whipped away in jeeps to the USAAF Officers' Mess. Refreshed by showers, we joined the Yanks for dinner and later spent an entertaining evening with them at the bar. The ACM was in great form and looked really fit. With proper respect for the temperature – Natal being only five degrees south of the Equator – he unfastened his tunic belt and buttons and, standing there with his hands in his pockets, swapped yarn for yarn. And did those Yanks love him for it! Even on such short acquaintance, they caught the enthusiasm for the man who was probably held in more genuine affection by his crews than any other British – or Allied – commander. During the course of the evening, we learned that we were going up to Washington, DC, via Georgetown and Nassau, and would use the North Atlantic route home, either direct or via Iceland. The news gave great satisfaction – what a trip it was going to be, and what scope for line-shooting when we arrived back at base! On the way to our sleeping quarters, we passed the tennis courts and were surprised to see several games in progress under floodlight. Some of

C-Charlie flying over the Amazon during the Special Mission to Brazil

the boys would have liked to 'have a bash' but we were scheduled for an early take-off on the morrow, so the wiser course of climbing into kip was taken.

Along our route from Natal to Georgetown lay the vast Amazonian jungle and as we flew over I felt that it must be the most awful place on earth. Even from the air, it looked evil and I had no wish to linger in the vicinity of those great, clawing fingers of trees which stretched in their millions as far as the eye could see. But as we crossed the coast, private fears were quickly forgotten in the thrill of seeing what I insisted on believing to be the longest river in the world. The Amazon – I was taught at school – rose in the Andes and flowed for 4,000 miles before it emptied into the Atlantic at the Equator; it was the longest river in the world. That was good enough for me, and no new-fangled 'Mississippi–Missouri' nonsense was going to make me change my mind! The heat in the cockpit was rather grim over the Equator, though we were all stripped to the waist in an effort to keep cool. Even 'C-Charlie' must have been feeling the effects, for he suddenly blew the Perspex out of the starboard window in the W/Op's compartment. I promptly plugged the hole with Tommy Greene's mosquito-net but an hour or so later that precious bundle followed the Perspex into the Atlantic.

'Baker' and 'Charlie' had been airborne eight-and-a-half hours when we touched down at Atkinson Field, Georgetown, and we were not only back on our own side of the Equator but also back in the Empire; though judging by the number of Yanks around to welcome us, one had doubts about it being 'British' Guiana. Although I had enjoyed the trip, I was not feeling too well and retired to bed immediately after dinner, in the hope that a good night's sleep would clear the trouble. When the boys returned later in the evening, I was in bad shape, so someone phoned for the MO, and when that gentleman arrived he took a very dim view of my condition. I was running a very high temperature and was beginning to ramble, so after dosing me with medicines and tablets, the doc left with the warning that I was to stay in bed for several days. Flying was entirely out of the question.

Despite the doc's orders and the pleading of the crew, I tottered down to a belated breakfast and, after toying with a cereal and a cup of coffee, I went round to sick quarters to plead my case. By a stroke of luck, a different MO was on duty and as soon as he saw my uniform he began to tell me about his life with the 8th Air Force in Lincolnshire. Seizing the opportunity, I told him that I had been stationed at Elsham Wolds and he began a long story about his visits to that station. It was a 'piece of cake'! With a parting promise to report sick at our next port-of-call, I got his OK to fly, nipped smartly away to collect my kit and went over to join the crew for the next leg of our tour.

By the time we crossed the coast, just short of Venezuela, and gained our operational height of 10,000 feet, my fever – or whatever it was – had almost disappeared and I was glad that I had decided to press on. As we flew over the island of Trinidad, I recalled that in pre-war days I had spent many happy hours working on the publication, *British West Indies Year Book* and over the years had become very interested in the places mentioned in the book, never dreaming that one day I would be flying in the vicinity of most of them. Out there, to starboard, were some of the places I had read about: Barbados; St Lucia; Dominica; Antigua; Barbuda and the Virgin Islands. As in the days of buccaneers and treasure-laden galleons, the air over the Caribbean still had the reputation of being treacherous but to us it was kind and we were able to concentrate on sightseeing, without risk of hurricane or sudden squall. Even from our altitude, the water looked as clear as crystal and the ocean bed could be seen for miles around each island, encircling them with great bands of mother-of-pearl. From Puerto Rico, we ran across a string of tiny islands – including Caicos Island and Turks Island – and, after an eight hour trip, finally touched down on the tree-fringed Windsor Field at Nassau, in the Bahamas.

Dinner at the Royal Victoria Hotel was a fitting climax to a delightful day. Served outdoors under the coconut palms, from which hung festoons of fairy lights, it was a meal to remember. And later, as we sipped iced drinks and smoked our cigarettes, a strolling native musician came to play local tunes on his guitar. It was an ideal set-up, as pleasant an evening as any I had spent for many a long year; but earthly paradises are so unreliable and Nassau proved no exception, for the starlit sky clouded over and when flashes of lightning and the distant rumble of thunder heralded the approach of a tropical storm, we scampered indoors. As I sat listening to the rain lashing against the gauze-covered windows, I recalled that rain had fallen at some of our other ports-of-call. At Rabat, I had just been informed by a RAF type that he had not seen rain for over a year, when a sudden shower sent him off to find shelter; at Bathurst, the heavens opened and we came off the runway like a flying boat; Recife greeted us with a downpour; our take-off from Georgetown was delayed because the rain came down so heavily that we could hardly see out of the cockpit windows; and now, at Nassau, we were getting the full treatment. I decided there and then that I would always treat travellers' tales of sun-drenched climes with a certain amount of reserve; there was nothing, I thought, quite so effective a debunking agent as a really good shower of rain, it helped one to maintain a sense of proportion.

After a short stay at Nassau, we took off for Bolling Field, Washington, DC. Less than five hours later, we had parked the Lancs. there and had jeeped to our rooms in the Visiting Officers' Quarters. One of the Army Air Force types who welcomed us was wearing the ribbon of the 1939–45 Star and we learned that before joining the 8th Air Force, he had done a tour of ops as a bomber pilot in the RAF. We lunched at the Officers' Club and, on retiring to the bar for a spot of fraternisation, found the local inhabitants in a state of considerable excitement. A second 'atomic' bomb had been dropped on Japan – at a place called Nagasaki – and the war, we were assured, was as good as won. Although still a little bit sceptical, we were beginning to realise that the Yanks really had unleashed a secret weapon of the first magnitude. It was fantastic that a nation geared for total warfare as Japan was, should be driven to ask for a 'cease fire' just because two bombs were dropped.

On 14 August 1945, several of the lads took off in a Dakota for a sightseeing tour of New York, whilst the rest of us elected to stay behind, some to spend a lazy day in the sun, and others to catch up on neglected correspondence. After lunch, I sent a cablegram to Dot and the folks at home, and then retired to bed for a sleep until dinner. At least, it was my intention to sleep until dinner but shortly after three o'clock, a couple of the boys came rushing into my room to tell me that the war was over. It was VJ Day!

When the lads returned from New York on the following day, we stay-at-homes regretted our decision to scrub round the trip, for they reported having had a marvellous time in the city. Arriving just after the VJ announcement, they were swept into Times Square and remained there until the early hours of the morning. Freddy Chandler was alleged to have been under the impression that the celebrations formed part of the city's welcome for the RAF but he soon found that the milling crowds were ready to cheer anyone wearing uniform. During the afternoon, we went down-town and found Washington surprisingly quiet for a capital; the main streets were almost deserted, shops were closed and shuttered, and we were lucky to find a place to dine. Back at the camp, we learned that the C-in-C had been invited to return to England, via Bermuda, in General Arnold's Douglas C.54 and, having accepted the invitation, had left instructions that we were to return at our leisure.

After four days in Washington, we took off from Bolling Field, turned north over the Potomac and set course for Dorval airport at Montreal, Canada. The airport is situated in flat country about ten miles from the city of Montreal, and as our Lancs. touched down on the long, concrete runway, I felt that I had arrived on hallowed ground. For it was from Dorval that thousands of aircraft had been ferried across the North Atlantic by crews of Transport Command. The first delivery flight of seven Lockheed Hudsons was made in the early winter of 1940, led by a certain Captain D.C.T. Bennett. On that memorable flight, the formation called at Gander and landed at Aldergrove, Northern Ireland; all seven aircraft arrived safely. I felt that I had connections – insignificant though they were – with the effort; for I had worked on ferried Hudsons at Aldergrove, had served under Air Vice-Marshal D.C.T. Bennett (one-time Captain, British Overseas Airways Corporation), and was at that moment taxying round the perimeter track of Dorval Airport. I knew that I was 'bending' the connection just a trifle, because Dorval had superseded St Hubert's Airport from which the take-off was actually made.

Arrangements had been made for us to stay at the Windsor Hotel, on Dominion Square, and after a quick shower and change of clothes, we sallied forth in search of an evening's entertainment. The Wingco, Blackie, Freddy, Tommy and I dined at an ultra-smart night-club known as 'El Morocco' and a pleasant time was had by all. So much did we enjoy the food, the dancing and the cabaret, that we were even able to laugh off the 25 per cent Federal Excise Tax and the five per cent Hospital Tax on our checks.

Our first full day in Montreal was spent rather quietly: we did a spot of shop-gazing and took in a couple of film shows. I was surprised at the strength of the French element in the city and at the extent to which the two languages were used in the normal course of business.

'Baker' and 'Charlie' were being given a 'forty-hour inspection' in readiness for the Atlantic crossing and when I went down to the maintenance hangar the following morning, I found the work well advanced and was assured by the Engineering Officer that the kites would be buttoned-up and ready to go within twenty-four hours. I was shown a signal regarding the automatic pilot, which rendered the system temporarily unserviceable, and agreed that the control-lever should be wired in the 'OFF' position, thus clearing the maintenance types. Anything which happened to the locking-wire afterwards was my own affair. Back in the city, I joined Freddy Shepherd for lunch, during which we decided to spend the afternoon on a circular tour. Like most big cities, Montreal still retained its electric trams and, having an extensive rail system, interposed special sightseeing jobs between the normal service trams; passengers being picked up at any point on the circuit and set down again at that spot after completing one lap. As the weather was delightful and the trams were open-air models, we had a very enjoyable ride. In the evening, I rejoined the crew as they set out in search of food, whipped on by the enthusiastic Blackie, who had received the hot tip that no one could claim to have visited Montreal unless he had dined at 'The Chicken Coop'. We soon located our target and entered a realm 'Where Chicken is King'. The restaurant was styled after the farmhouses of the West, with rough-hewn tables and chairs, crossed pitchforks for hatracks, walls decorated with Western scenes, and waitresses dressed demurely in check aprons with hair-ribbons to match. In my ignorance, I had thought that chicken was roasted, boiled or fried, but the menu taught me that a chicken could be cooked in a hundred different ways. Being sticklers for convention, we settled for roast chicken. We got roast chicken. Not slices or portions but one whacking great chicken on each plate! There was a notice on the wall which read,

'Don't fidget and struggle with knife and fork,
Use your fingers – we won't talk!'

and, taking our cue from that invitation and from neighbouring diners, we went native for one evening.

A knowledge of Western slang and a ready wit were essential to a proper appreciation of 'The Chicken Coop', as was quickly realised by one embarrassed member of our party who discovered, too late, that the little room with 'MAW' on the door was no place for gentlemen.

Our four days in Montreal had been thoroughly enjoyable and we were loath to leave, but the inspection on 'Baker' and 'Charlie' had been completed and there was no reasonable excuse for prolonging our stay. Financially, it was advisable to depart without delay, for we were no longer guests of a Government and the mounting hotel bills and the cost-of-living were making rapid inroads into our dollar resources. We coached to Dorval and, in a very short time, were making our circuit over the 'drome and setting course for Gander Airport, Newfoundland. As we crossed the St Lawrence River, I thought fondly of our brief meeting with the Canadians at home; and of the phrase which one heard everywhere in the city of Montreal, 'You're welcome!'

Even in the glory of a summer's day, Gander Airport looked desolate and I could well imagine that in mid-winter it would be a good place to be posted from. Built on a lumber-clearing on the north-east coast of Newfoundland, it was set in a landscape of swamps and small lakes, interspersed with scrub country and low hills. There were no roads to the outer world and everything had to be flown in or flown out. Amenities at the camp had doubtless improved over the years but we found the five hours we spent there quite sufficient.

At ten minutes past midnight, the engines of the two Lancasters stirred into life and after a quick check round the cockpit – sparing a glance for my mascot, 'Joe' – I gave the thumbs-up sign to the Wingco, who smiled an acknowledgement and rolled 'Charlie' on to the perimeter track, to take up position behind Calder in 'Baker'. Turning into wind and making a final intercom. check of the crew and passengers, the skipper waited for his 'green' and then opened up for the take-off.

We had just got off the deck when we heard Jock Calder call control and tell them he had feathered one of 'Baker's' engines and was coming in to land. Poor Jock! He had been dogged by engine-trouble, twice in 'Abel', and now in 'Baker', and it seemed that he might be in for a lengthy stay at Gander. Still, it was a lot healthier to lose an engine in the circuit at Gander than at some point in mid-Atlantic. We extended sympathy and headed for the coast, hoping that 'Baker's' trouble was not infectious. As the last pinheads of light from the airport faded into the darkness, we lost contact with the New World; ahead, lay the Atlantic Ocean, and – if all went well – breakfast in Prestwick, Scotland.

Taking turns at the controls, the Wingco and I nursed 'Charlie' through the night and our navigators kept us informed of progress. We were at 9,000 feet, cruising at a steady 155 knots, the fuel position (standard tanks only) was quite satisfactory and our four Merlins were bang-on.

When Freddie Chandler started passing revised ETAs we began to realise that the Met. wind-forecasts had been too optimistic and that we were – as Blackie put it – 'Getting nowhere, fast!' After ten-and-a-half hours flying, we had still not sighted land and with lots of low cloud rolling in to obscure the view, this had to be the time when Tommy Greene's set chose to go U/S and he was unable to contact Prestwick. With very little fuel left in the tanks, we eventually picked up the Scottish coastline, pinpointed our position and made for the airport. We lobbed down in pouring rain, with visibility practically nil, and when I snapped up the engine cut-off switches after a quick running-down check, 'Charlie's' engines had been running continuously for eleven hours fifteen minutes – our actual airborne time being ten minutes short of eleven hours.

After all the long flights we had made, the trip from Prestwick to Wyton was but a short hop. To announce our arrival, we did a modest beat-up of the 'drome before coming in to land, and by the time we had taxied on to the grass at the side of the control-tower, a crowd had assembled to give us a welcome. Peter Clayton – who had been in charge during the Wingco's absence – was waiting for us in the watch-office; as was a Customs Officer, to whom we 'declared' 200 'Sweet Caporal' cigarettes – which were duty-free, anyhow! We gathered our bags and drove to the Mess for dinner, to be faced with a barrage of questions from the boys of the squadron. Later in the

Crew of A-Abel for the Special Mission to Brazil. From left to right: the author, Tommy Greene, 'Blackie' Blackadder, 'Mac' McFarlane (seated), Freddy Chandler, 'Wingco' Craig and Johnny Cooper

evening, we were guests at a private party given by the Station Commander, Group Captain Eayrs. To our sorrow, the party was also the occasion of our farewell to Colonel Hecksher, and we all expressed gratitude for the very big part he had played in the success of the mission.

Jock Calder and crew arrived in 'B-Baker' during the afternoon of the following day, their engine-trouble having been of a minor character. As I watched the kite taxi into position alongside 'Charlie', I felt very proud of our two 'white elephants' – as I had heard an engine-fitter call them on the morning before we left Wyton – and though the sand, dust and rain of many countries had dulled the original, resplendent black-and-white finish, they still looked like thoroughbreds and, throughout the trip of over 17,000 miles, they had performed like thoroughbreds.

From beginning to end, the Special Mission to Brazil had been the sort of trip that people dream about but never seriously believe could possibly come true. In the month that had passed since we took off from St Mawgan, there had been enough excitement and interest to provide material for a lifetime's line-shooting and happy memories of good friends and good times which would improve – like good wine – with the years.

CHAPTER EIGHT

OPERATION 'BOWLER HAT'

It was great to see the three-engined wizard again and, as I went over to shake hands, I gave an undignified whoop of delight. I had imagined Freddy Keeler sweating it out on trips over the 'hump' and was not slow to point out that I had endured many a sleepless night, wondering if he had survived the war in the east. When I learned that the overseas posting had not materialised, that my sympathy had been wasted on a man who had strayed no further than Bushey Park, I protested that I might have been kept better informed.

Although it was only three months since Freddy left the squadron, many events of mutual interest had taken place and discussion of these merited my warning Brooky that I was taking the afternoon off. After exchanging news of our respective spouses, we turned to flying topics and, as Freddy had little to report, talk was mostly about the squadron. I told of postings, promotions, gongs, and of the 'Dodge' and 'Liberty' trips which were still keeping the boys airborne. As I had flown on a 'Liberty' trip the previous day, I was able to give Freddy first-hand information. The heavies were being used to ferry leave-expired bods back to Germany, returning with luckier types just starting their leave. I flew with Kelly in 'P-Peter' and our destination was Nuremberg, a city I had visited on two previous occasions, though in rather different circumstances. On arrival, we deposited our passengers on the tarmac in front of the wrecked hangars and then jeeped into town for lunch. It was an uncanny feeling, riding through streets I had helped to bomb and I half expected to see accusing fingers pointing in my direction. But there was no evidence of animosity and when we arrived at the American Forces Canteen, we found ourselves being served, efficiently and pleasantly, by German waitresses. From our window-seats, we could see little knots of German children gathered round Yanks in the street, probably asking the question which had become a universal quip, 'Got any gum, chum?' But I was not happy in Nuremberg, I could not shake off thoughts of that night when ninety-six of our aircraft were smacked down during a raid on the city; and I was glad when we made our way back to the 'drome, collected our passengers and departed.

The 'Dodge' trips were also ferrying efforts but the traffic was one-way, as the passengers were mostly Army types who were being flown from Italy to England for demob; the picking-up points were Naples and Bari. Unfortunately, I had not clicked for a trip, chiefly because I was free-lancing again and keen competition between crews for a place on the 'battle-order' ruled out any chance of muscling-in as a spare bod. However, I had just thrown in my lot with Flying Officer Doolan's crew and expected to be giving my tropical kit another airing during the following week.

As a change from squadron gen, I told Freddy about my ASR course at Calshot and then mentioned the letters I had received from Jimmy Green, Steve and Bill Bailey – three lads he had never met but with whose names and histories he was familiar. Jimmy was full of emigration plans and eager to try his luck in South Africa or Rhodesia, though he harboured doubts about being accepted because of his low medical category. Steve had written from India to say that he anticipated an early return to UK; he had never really settled down at Mauripur and was probably still pining for the days at Aldergrove with the Met. Flight. The letter from Bill Bailey brought news of the old 'W-for-William' crew. Bill was Briefing Officer at Northolt, after a spell of duty with 45 Group, based at Montreal; Corky was stationed at Banff, in Scotland, as Airfield Controller; Reg Boys was flying with Transport Command; Eddie, of course, had returned to Canada; and, according to rumour, Doug was dicing somewhere in the Far East; of our skipper, Reg, there was nothing to report, except that Bill had heard that he was a Flight Lieutenant.

Saving the tastiest bit of news till the last, I gave Freddy a rough outline of the Brazil trip, illustrating my description by means of photographs which Blackie had taken during the trip. Unable to resist a little line-shooting, I turned the lapel of my tunic to show Freddy my 'Bellows Club' badge, which had arrived that very morning by Air Mail, from the Vice-Consul at Natal. It was, I believed, the only Bellows Club badge in Britain. Whilst on the topic, I had to tell of a matter which gave grounds for a private moan amongst the boys. The FAB lads confided that the Brazilians wished to decorate each aircrew member of the party with the Order of the Southern Cross but that the powers-that-be in England had ordained that the decoration be restricted to pilots only. Whatever the truth of the matter, we cast many an envious glance at the beautiful blue ribbon displayed on the Wingco's tunic. To round off the story of the trip, I was able to bring Freddy bang-up-to-date with news of the third Lanc., for Jock Cairns had returned only the previous day, having flown 'Abel' home from Rio by way of the West Indies, Canada and Iceland. Jock brought back newsreels of our visit and the squadron was looking forward to seeing them at the local cinemas.

As always happens when old friends meet, time travelled at full boost and revs, and long before we had exhausted our topics of conversation, Freddy had to rush away to catch his train back to base. Fortunately, Brooky was going down to Huntingdon in the Jaguar, so he ran Freddy and me to the railway station, thereby enabling us to say our farewells over a leisurely cup of char in the refreshment room. I had thoroughly enjoyed the visit of my old 'oppo' and, as I waggled a vigorous thumb in the direction of the fast-disappearing south-bound train, I wondered if I would ever see Freddy again. Our days in the Royal Air Force were numbered and the return to Civvy Street would doubtless bring its own problems, which might conspire to foil our plans for reunions over the years. But that was in the lap of the gods and, whatever happened, I could never be robbed of my memories of Freddy Keeler; he had been a true friend and had been one of the most conscientious blokes who ever lifted a Lanc. off a runway.

It was no use pretending to myself that I liked the idea of flying without a parachute, because I didn't. Of course, I had flown dozens of times without one but only on training trips of short duration; the trip to Italy was a very different kettle of fish. The mileage over land would be considerable and landing grounds not easily found in an emergency; in addition, I still considered that the average squadron engines were pretty grim compared with the engines of wartime days. However, the fact remained that on Operation 'Dodge', the return trip would be made with a complement of Army bods and as they would not be carrying 'chutes, we were to show our sporting spirit by leaving our own 'chutes behind in the locker room. As a gesture, we would be carrying Mae Wests for passengers and crew. This was not the only strange note struck at the Dodge briefing, for the crews themselves looked unfamiliar in khaki drill, liberally sprinkled in the vicinity of the pockets with yellow powder from the mepacrine tablets, which had been issued to prevent something-or-other. Strict instructions were given that on arrival at our destination, tarpaulin sheets were to be affixed over the dinghy stowage in the mainplane, to prevent the heat of the sun prematurely discharging the contents of the CO_2 bottle and inflating the dinghy: the fuel state was to be carefully checked before return and only enough fuel taken on board as would safely enable the aircraft to reach base: and, finally, we were to avoid eating or drinking anywhere except in the Mess or in a Forces canteen.

As I climbed into 'R-Roger' to make my checks, I shuddered at the sight of painted circles, each containing a number, disfiguring the fuselage floor. Obviously a sop to appease the Army's appetite for doing things by numbers. Paddy Doolan was not visibly affected but I brooded for a long time, only suppressing my better feelings in the interests of load distribution and safety, and accepting the necessity for the circles which indicated passenger seating positions. With 'Joe' installed at his usual station, all checks made and the four Merlins straining at the throttles, I thumbed an OK for taxiing and 'Roger' rolled out of dispersal for the long trip to Sunny Italy.

After a pleasant stooge over France, we crossed the coast between Marseilles and Toulon, then turned east for the run along the French Riviera. Cannes, Nice, Monte Carlo and Menton had doubtless lost much of their former gaiety but the view of their surroundings still looked lovely from the air. From a background of wooded hills – tinted golden-brown by the early autumn – sleek, white buildings staggered in refreshing disorder to the beaches, there to be halted by the blue waters of the Mediterranean. It made a delightful picture in the bright September sunshine. The next point of interest on our route was Corsica and I was amazed at the rugged nature of the island. Reference to the navigator's maps showed that one of the peaks, Monte Cinto, was almost 9,000 feet high, and that was quite a useful height for a European mountain. Turning south over Elba, we took a peek at the romantic island of Monte Cristo and then closed in to the coast of Italy, which was followed until we altered course over the Bay of Naples. The crew were enraptured by the beauty of Naples – with the Isle of Capri and Vesuvius thrown in for good measure – whilst I, fresh from Rio, conceded that the view was not entirely without merit. A quick crossing of the Apennines and we were soon letting-down to join the circuit at Bari, doing a crafty turn over the Adriatic – just for the line-book.

Seven hours after leaving Wyton, we had parked 'Roger' in the serried ranks of erstwhile bombers and, after reporting a very sick port-inner engine to the ground staff, plodded along to the Mess for a wash and then in to dinner.

The sick engine proved to be beyond repair by the facilities available and we were faced with the alternative of flying back as passengers or waiting until another kite went U/S, so that one of its engines could be whipped out to make 'Roger' serviceable. We had no desire to return to base as passengers. Our kite was still U/S when our third day at Bari was enlivened by the arrival of another bunch of '156' boys, to whom we had to explain our continued presence, when our fellow-'Dodgers' were half-way home with their loads of brown jobs.

The main item of news from the boys came as a shock. The squadron was breaking up! We could hardly be blamed for doubting the statement, for rumour had broken up the squadron at least a dozen times since the end of the war; but the boys assured us that this was no rumour, it was cast-iron gen.

Next day, an early-morning message from the 'drome bore good tidings for Doolan's crew; an aircraft of another squadron was available and we were scheduled to take off after breakfast. Down at the 'drome, we found our passengers already assembled near the entrance-door of 'Q-Queenie' and, after transferring our kit from 'Roger', we introduced ourselves and gave them instructions for the trip. Whilst the kitbags and equipment of the soldiers were being stowed away in the bomb-bay panniers by the ground staff, we fitted the Army boys with Mae Wests and assured the nervous types that flying was a piece of cake. With everyone safely on board and each yellow circle obliterated by a khaki-clad posterior, I started the engines and gave Paddy the OK. Because of the tight parking and the sandy nature of the ground, the customary run-up was dispensed with and we trundled away at low revs to take up position behind the long line of aircraft waiting to take off. When our turn came, we did a snap check of the engines and then opened-up as the preceding kite left the deck. In a very short time we too were airborne and, with a last look at the Adriatic, turned on to course. Like the troopship leaving Bombay, in the words of an old RAF song, we also were 'heavily laden with time-expired men'.

Shortly after leaving Bari, we ran into heavy cloud and even when we climbed to cross the Apennines we were still 'shipping water' and the bods in the bomb aimer's compartment were getting wet.

The cloud was thick and we could not climb over it because the passengers were not equipped with oxygen masks. The weather must have been pretty bad in some areas because we heard several pilots calling Bari and announcing their intention of returning. Rather than disappoint our Army lads, who were settling down nicely after their initial nervousness, we decided to press on and were rewarded by an early break in the cloud, which we found by flying south of track. Over the Mediterranean, conditions were ideal and spirits brightened considerably. A huge tin of toffee was passed round by one of the privates and some of the more venturesome souls moved up to the cockpit to see the crew at work. We had been 'in George' for quite a time and when Paddy moved out of his seat so that I could take over for a spell, we stood chatting in the gangway, while 'Queenie' flew on, apparently pilotless. The Army lads' faces were a study in surprise and discomfiture, and after Paddy and I had satisfied our sense of humour by lingering for longer than was strictly necessary, I climbed into the driver's seat and explained the automatic pilot system to one or two interested types.

Seven hours thirty minutes after leaving Bari, we touched down at Tibenham and, after discharging our passengers and cargo, took off again for the short trip back to base.

Some time after our 'Dodge' flight, we flew over to Tuddenham for an exercise in conjunction with the Ground Control Approach (GCA) people there. The thing that interested me most was not the GCA exercise, neither was it the three-engined take-off we made on our return to base after completing the exercise; it was the jet-engined Gloster Meteor fighter we found parked alongside 'N-Nan' when we returned from lunch to continue our circuits and GCA-bumps. The Meteor was the first 'squirt job' I had seen at close quarters and, for that reason alone, deserved a place in my memory. As I gazed at its propless motors and stubby undercarriage, and compared them with the Hydromatic 'fans' and lengthy oleo-legs of the Lancaster, I felt that I was standing at the crossroads of aviation; that aircraft as I knew them were already obsolete, though likely to drag on for a few years. Much as I hated the thought, I realised that my beloved Lancasters and Merlins would appear just as ancient and cumbersome to the next generation as the biplanes and rotaries of the '14–'18 war had appeared to my generation.

The Meteor was the complete answer to the rumours which had circulated at Gloucester when I was down there on my fitter's course, during the early part of 1941. Several of my fellow-trainees swore that they had seen a propless single-engined fighter flying in the vicinity of the camp but the idea was so absurd that little attention was paid to the stories. The supporting rumour that this mysterious aircraft had an out-of-this-world exhaust-note, was treated with equal scorn. From time to time similar rumours had cropped up but it was not until I arrived at Seighford in 1943 that I really believed in the existence of jet-engines. There, I heard and saw a Wellington flying with a jet-engine installed somewhere on the aircraft – poor visibility prevented me from seeing exactly where. During 1944 and 1945, the jet-engine made great strides and was obviously destined to be the aero-engine of the future. Unfortunately for Britain, the Germans had been working on similar and even on more advanced lines, and had produced jet and rocket-propelled aircraft, the pilotless V1 flying bomb, and the V2 rocket bomb.

The first week of October, 1945, was one of the happiest and, at the same time, one of the saddest weeks of my life in the RAF. It was happy because I went home on a 'week-end' to see my wife and our brand-new daughter Marion; and because I took the news that I would be demobbed in a month's time. It was sad because during that week, 156 Squadron ceased to exist. Brooky, Bash and many more old comrades had been posted to Transport Command; others had 'gone redundant'; some – like myself – were waiting for *der Tag*, whilst the remainder had opted to stand by Wingco Craig who was to take command of the re-formed 35 Squadron at Gravely. The Wingco was choosing his own key men from '156' and had made a good start with 'Shorty' Harris as Flight Commander, 'Tiger' Kennedy as Navigation Officer, 'Buzz' Walton as Signals Leader, and Johnny Cooper as Gunnery Leader. He urged me to extend my service for a further period of eighteen months and accept the position of Flight Engineer Leader with the new squadron. It was a great opportunity and a great temptation, for I would be promoted to Flight Lieutenant, with a substantial increase in rate of pay, and would be able to continue my association with many old friends and with the good old Lancs. The Wingco was very persuasive and if I had been a single man there would have been no hesitation. But I was married, with a week-old baby, and I felt that my first duty – now the war was over – was to my wife and family; with my feet planted firmly on the deck.

It was during that week, also, that I learned of a very interesting coincidence. An American Superfortress – the first to visit Britain – was scheduled to touch down at one of our 'dromes, *en route* for the Continent, and Wingco Craig was one of those invited to inspect the aircraft. He went down by car and after looking round the Superfort, was just starting his engine for the return trip, when he heard someone frantically calling his name. A staff-car had stopped nearby on the perimeter-track and from it emerged a smartly-uniformed figure, which made good speed across the intervening grass, bellowing at intervals, 'CRAIG!' 'CRAIG!!' As the Wingco stepped out of his car, the energetic one arrived and promptly flung himself into a fond embrace with the startled Craig. It was Umberto! After a brief interlude of the 'Well, I'll be damned!' sort of conversation – which conveys little, but enables one to recover from initial surprise – the Wingco learned that Umberto had been appointed to a position on the Brazilian Air Attaché's staff in Washington, DC, and when the Superfort trip was mooted he had been invited to take part in the mission. He was returning to the aircraft when he spotted the Wingco getting into his car and had been afraid that he would have been unable to attract the Wingco's attention before he moved off. I was delighted to learn that all was well with our good friend, Umberto, and wished that I could have been there to greet him.

Following my decision to take my release, I was posted to Station Headquarters and attached to the Lancaster Servicing Squadron Test Flight. As there was very little air-testing to be done, I was practically at a loose end and, apart from one or two spells of duty as Orderly Officer, spent most of my time sorting out my kit and writing to advise friends of pending change of address. I was no longer happy in my work and when the boys of 156 Squadron moved out, taking their aircraft with them, I could think of nothing but my release. Fortunately, I had Blackie Blackadder, Freddy Chandler, Peter Clayton and Tommy Greene for company; the two navigators waiting for the release of Group 23, the ex-Master Bomber and the wireless operator waiting for their posting notices. It was the end of yet another chapter in my life as a Bomber Boy.

The date of our release – Operation 'Bowler Hat', as Freddy Chandler called it – was fixed for 3 November 1945. We were to report at Uxbridge for the purpose of signing ourselves out of active service and into Civvy Street; and at Wembley for the issue of civilian clothing. But that date was three weeks ahead and I had no wish to spend the intervening period on a station from which the life-blood had been drained away, so I had a heart-to-heart chat with the Station

Adjutant – an understanding type – and wangled fourteen days' leave; subject to my having handed-in my flying kit and 'cleared' the station.

The disposal of my flying kit was not a pleasant business and as each item was checked off against my flying clothing book, my spirits sank lower and lower. Everything had to go. My cosy helmet, the over-long but extra-warm white sweater, goggles, gloves, the outer-suit I seldom wore, and the long underwear I never wore, even the plated whistle which had dangled from the port side of my battle-blouse. Most of all, I hated to part with my flying boots. It would, I thought, be a fine gesture if the RAF allowed every aircrew type to retain his flying boots, for they were counted amongst his most treasured possessions – in many cases, third only to his flying log-book and his mascot.

Having disposed of my flying kit, I decided to take all my personal stuff home and spent the rest of the morning packing my travelling trunk and zip bag, and wondering what the future had in store for me. I wondered how I would settle down to civilian life and what conditions would be encountered in the post-war years.

During lunch, Peter Clayton brought welcome news. He had been asked to air-test a '156' kite, 'J-Jig', which had been left at Wyton for inspection – he wondered if we would care to make up a crew. Just like that! If we would *care* to make up a crew. We would almost have begged on bended knees for the chance! Tommy Greene organised helmets from the Signals Section, whilst Blackie, Freddy and I collected 'chutes and harness, and then we hurried over to the Maintenance Hangar before any interfering types had time to change their minds.

It was a glorious afternoon and as we turned on to course, after doing a circuit of the 'drome, I felt the old thrill of flying surge through me – just as it had done on my very first Lancaster trip from Lindholme. Strangely enough, I never quite got the same thrill when flying in any aircraft other than a Lanc. Flips in Hudsons, Blenheims, Halifaxes, Wellingtons and the like, were enjoyable but the old Lancs had that little extra something that the others hadn't got. Certainly, I had every reason to be grateful for my association with the 'Queen of the Skies'; I had completed fifty-four successful sorties and two abortive sorties – with an operational flying time of over 320 hours – without so much as receiving a scratch; and that in a Command which lost on operations more than 7,000 aircraft and suffered 75,000 casualties in a little over three years.

We had been airborne for just over an hour when we sighted the Wyton water-tower and in a few minutes we were making our approach; wheels down and locked, full flap coming on, engine-note rising as the props went to fully-fine, and 'Jig' nicely lined-up on the runway; I cut back the throttles as we crossed the boundary and Peter rolled her in with the merest trace of tyre scream. With side-windows open to flush out the fuselage with the fresh, autumn breeze, we trundled merrily round the perimeter track, to fetch up with a squeal of brakes in front of the hangar.

I made a prolonged running-down check, for old times sake, and then – with the final 'plops' of the four Merlins for a swan-song – I murmured a prayer of thanks for countless blessings received, collected my mascot 'Joe' and retired, with my ghosts and my memories, from the stage of military aviation.

Appendix 1

FLIGHT ENGINEER'S DUTIES

Extract from A.M.O. A.538/1943.

The duties and responsibilities of Flight Engineers are as follows :—

(i) To operate certain controls at the engineer's station and watch appropriate gauges as indicated in the relevant publications.

(ii) In certain types of aircraft, to act as pilot's assistant to the extent of being able to fly straight and level and on a course.

(iii) To advise the captain of the aircraft as to the functioning of the engines and the fuel, oil and coolant systems, both before and during flight.

(iv) To ensure effective liaison between the captain of the aircraft and the maintenance staff by communicating to the latter such technical notes regarding the performance and maintenance of the aircraft in flight as may be required.

(v) **To carry out practicable emergency repairs during flight.**

(vi) To act as stand-by air gunner.

Flight Engineer's Duties

179

APPENDIX 2

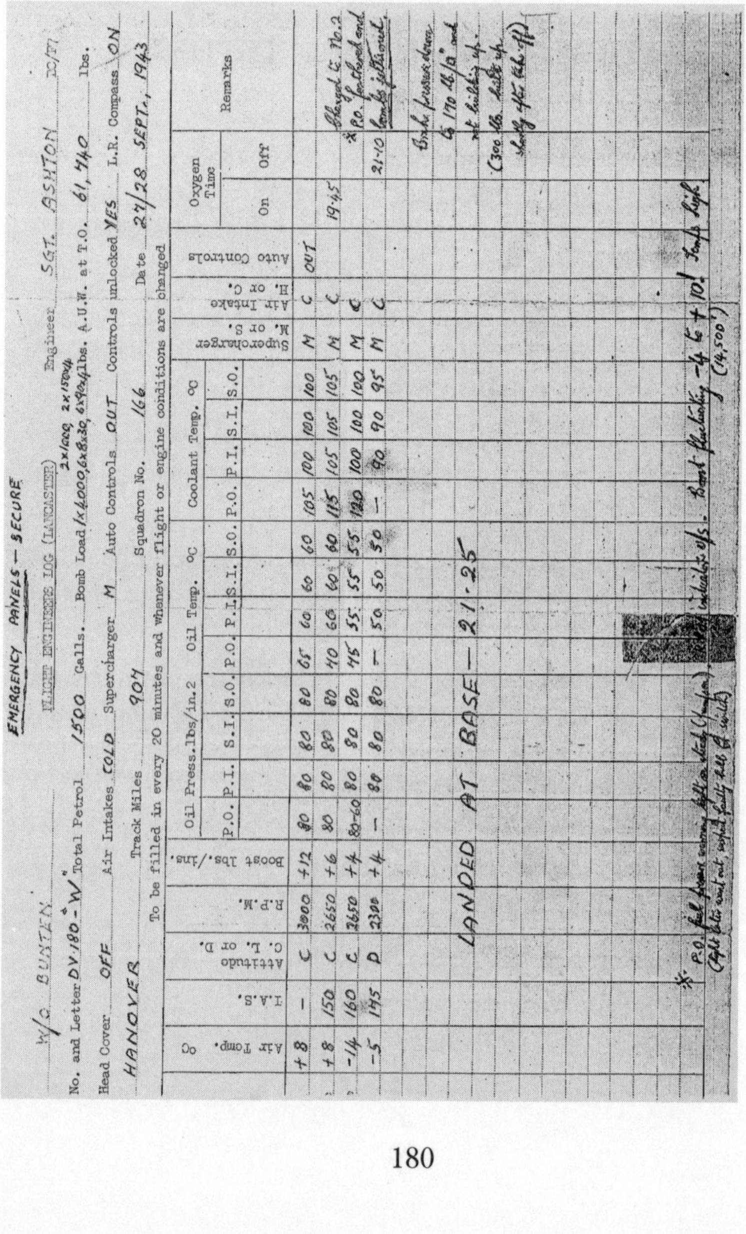

EMERGENCY PANELS — SECURE

W/C BUNTEN   FLIGHT ENGINEERS LOG (LANCASTER)   Engineer SGT. ASHTON   DC/F7

No. and Letter DV.180 – "W" Total Petrol 1500 Galls. Bomb Load 1x4000, 6x8x30, 6x90x4 (2x1000, 2x150x4) lbs. A.U.W. at T.O. 61,740 lbs.

Head Cover OFF Air Intakes COLD Supercharger M Auto Controls OUT Controls unlocked YES L.R. Compass ON

HANOVER Track Miles 907 Squadron No. 166 Date 27/28 SEPT., 1943

To be filled in every 20 minutes and whenever flight or engine conditions are changed

Air Temp. °C	I.A.S.	Attitude C. L. or D.	R.P.M.	Boost lbs./ins.	Oil Press. lbs/in.2 P.O.	P.I.	S.I.	S.O.	Oil Temp. °C P.O.	P.I.	S.I.	S.O.	Coolant Temp. °C P.O.	P.I.	S.I.	S.O.	Supercharger M. or S.	Air Intake H. or C.	Auto Controls	Oxygen Time On	Off	Remarks
+8	–	C	3000	+12	80	80	80	80	65	60	60	60	105	100	100	100	M	C	OUT			
+8	150	C	2650	+6	80	80	80	80	40	60	60	60	115	105	105	105	M	C		19.45		Changed E. No.2
-14	160	C	2650	+4	80-60	80	80	80	45	55	55	55	120	100	100	100	M	C				* P.O. feathered and
-5	175	D	2300	+4	–	80	80	80	–	50	50	50	–	90	90	95	M	C			21.10	bombs jettisoned.

Brake pressure down to 170 lb/□" and not building up. (300 lbs. built up shortly after take-off)

LANDED AT BASE — 21.25

* P.O. fuel pressure warning light on steady (pump). (Light later went out, suspect faulty bulb of switch). [illegible] indicator u/s. Boost fluctuating -4 to +10! (14,500') Temps high.

Flight Engineer's Log 27/28 September, 1943

APPENDIX 3

Date	No. of Hour sorties	Aircraft Type and No.	Pilot	Duty	Remarks (including results of bombing, gunnery, exercises, etc.)	Day	Night
					Time carried forward ►	36·20	54·45
		LANCASTER					
1-7-43		"S" - ED451	F/SGT BUNTEN	FLIGHT ENGINEER	N.F.T.	1·00	
3-7-43	7	"Z" - EE196	" "	"	COLOGNE		5·45
4-7-43		"W" - DV180	"	"	AIR TEST	·30	
5-7-43		"	"	"	N.F.T.	·40	
6-7-43		"	"	"	AIR/SEA FIRING	1·00	
6-7-43	8	"	"	"	MINELAYING - GIRONDE RIVER		6·10
8-7-43		"	"	"	FIGHTER AFFILIATION	·40	
8-7-43	9	"	"	"	COLOGNE		5·40
9-7-43	10	"	"	"	GELSENKIRCHEN		6·15
12-7-43		"	"	"	N.F.T.	·20	
12-7-43	11	"	"	"	TURIN		10·05
14-7-43		"	W/O BUNTEN	"	N.F.T.	·45	
16-7-43		"	"	"	FORMATION FLYING	1·10	
18-7-43		"	"	"	FORMATION FLYING -	1·30	
24-7-43		"	"	"	N.F.T.	·40	
24-7-43		"	"	"	HAMBURG		5·40
27-7-43	12	"	"	"	N.F.T.	·40	
29-7-43		"	"	"	HAMBURG		5·10
29-7-43	13	"	"	"	REMSCHEID (Blamed no 3 engine, 30 on fire)		5·00
30-7-43	14	"Y" ED731	"	"			
					Total Time	45·15	104·30

Flying Log Book 1 July 1943 – 30 July 1943

APPENDIX 4

BOMBER COMMAND FLIGHT ENGINEER LOG.

'A' TO BE COMPLETED BEFORE FLIGHT:—

CAPTAIN:— F/LT. DENVER	F/ENGINEER:— F/O ASHTON	BOMB LOAD:— 7,200 lbs.	TOTAL FUEL:— 2,100 gls.	A.U.W.:— 63,820 lbs.
DATE:— 4/4/45	AIRCRAFT TYPE:— LANCASTER	MK. III	AIRCRAFT No:— ME.368	LETTER:— F

'B' CHECK BEFORE FLIGHT:—

ITEM	INITIALS	ITEM	INITIALS
PITOT HEAD COVER OFF	J.W.A.	ESCAPE HATCHES SECURE	J.W.A.
STATIC VENT PLUGS OUT	J.W.A.	CONTROLS UNLOCKED	J.W.A.
NITROGEN SYSTEM ON	—	AUTO-CONTROLS (CLUTCHES IN)	J.W.A.
SUPERCHARGER 'M' GEAR	J.W.A.	D.R. COMPASS ON	J.W.A.
AIR INTAKES (COLD)	J.W.A.	GILL OR RAD. POSITION Open or Closed	AUTO
BRAKE PRESSURE BEFORE 'CHOCKS AWAY'	280 Lbs/□	BRAKE PRESSURE AFTER LANDING	40 Lbs/□

'C' TO BE COMPLETED AFTER FLIGHT:—

TIME TO NEAREST MINUTE OF :—

START UP	21·40 Hrs.	SWITCH OFF	05·10 Hrs.	TOTAL RUNNING TIME	7·30 Hrs.
TAKE-OFF	21·50 Hrs.	TOUCH DOWN	05·00 Hrs.	TIME AIRBORNE	7·10 Hrs.
SET COURSE	22·07 Hrs.	OVER BASE	04·50 Hrs.	TIME ON COURSE	6·45 Hrs.

TARGET:— LUTZKENDORF (DEPUTY MASTER BOMBER)	SQUADRON:— 156 (PATHFINDER FORCE)

'D' FUEL ANALYSIS :—

ITEM	FUEL USED	FUEL LEFT	AIR MILES	TRACK MILES	A.M.P.G.	T.M.P.G.	G.P.H.
F/ENGINEER	1490 Gls.	610 Gls.	1330	1233·5	0·98	0·91	205
F/ENGINEER LDR	Gls.	Gls.					

'E' REMARKS :— BY F/ENGINEER.

```
       AVERAGE T.A.S. — 194 KNOTS
   FUEL USED ON COURSE — 1363
        "      TAXYING  —  20
        "      CIRCLING —  77
        "      TAKE-OFF —  30
   "GEORGE" TIME — 3 HRS.
                    (MAGS — not checked)
x Nav's blackout curtain U/S
:: S.O. up to 3,200 revs on T.O.
x brake pressure down to 40 in dispersal
```

REMARKS :— BY F/ENGINEER LDR.

```
    .
  29·40
  21·40
  7·30 hrs.
```

LOG COMPLETE :— J. Norman Ashton F/O
F/ENGINEER

LOG CHECKED :— _____
F/ENGINEER LDR.

Flight Engineer's Log 4 April 1945

INDEX